Scaling Customer Success

Building the Customer Success Center of Excellence

Chitra Madhwacharyula
Shreesha Ramdas

Scaling Customer Success: Building the Customer Success Center of Excellence

Chitra Madhwacharyula
Saratoga, CA, USA

Shreesha Ramdas
Saratoga, CA, USA

ISBN-13 (pbk): 978-1-4842-9191-7
https://doi.org/10.1007/978-1-4842-9192-4

ISBN-13 (electronic): 978-1-4842-9192-4

Copyright © 2023 by Chitra Madhwacharyula, Shreesha Ramdas

This work is subject to copyright. All rights are reserved by the Publisher, whether the whole or part of the material is concerned, specifically the rights of translation, reprinting, reuse of illustrations, recitation, broadcasting, reproduction on microfilms or in any other physical way, and transmission or information storage and retrieval, electronic adaptation, computer software, or by similar or dissimilar methodology now known or hereafter developed.

Trademarked names, logos, and images may appear in this book. Rather than use a trademark symbol with every occurrence of a trademarked name, logo, or image we use the names, logos, and images only in an editorial fashion and to the benefit of the trademark owner, with no intention of infringement of the trademark.

The use in this publication of trade names, trademarks, service marks, and similar terms, even if they are not identified as such, is not to be taken as an expression of opinion as to whether or not they are subject to proprietary rights.

While the advice and information in this book are believed to be true and accurate at the date of publication, neither the authors nor the editors nor the publisher can accept any legal responsibility for any errors or omissions that may be made. The publisher makes no warranty, express or implied, with respect to the material contained herein.

    Managing Director, Apress Media LLC: Welmoed Spahr
    Acquisitions Editor: Shiva Ramachandran
    Development Editor: James Markham
    Coordinating Editor: Jessica Vakili

Distributed to the book trade worldwide by Springer Science+Business Media New York, 1 New York Plaza, New York, NY 10004. Phone 1-800-SPRINGER, fax (201) 348-4505, e-mail orders-ny@springer-sbm.com, or visit www.springeronline.com. Apress Media, LLC is a California LLC and the sole member (owner) is Springer Science + Business Media Finance Inc (SSBM Finance Inc). SSBM Finance Inc is a **Delaware** corporation.

For information on translations, please e-mail booktranslations@springernature.com; for reprint, paperback, or audio rights, please e-mail bookpermissions@springernature.com.

Apress titles may be purchased in bulk for academic, corporate, or promotional use. eBook versions and licenses are also available for most titles. For more information, reference our Print and eBook Bulk Sales web page at http://www.apress.com/bulk-sales.

Printed on acid-free paper

We dedicate this book to the Customer Success community and, in particular, to the innovative thought leaders and practitioners who are at the forefront of the Customer Success 3.0 revolution towards standardization, scale and customer led growth. Your passion, expertise, and dedication to Customer Success has inspired us. Thank you for your contributions.

Table of Contents

About the Authors xi

Acknowledgments xiii

Foreword xv

Introduction xvii

Chapter 1: Customer Success Center of Excellence (CS CoE) 1

Customer Success CoE Functions 3
    Core Functions 4
    Extended Functions 5
    CS Digital Engagement Strategy 8
How to Build a CS CoE Organization 9
    From Theory to Practice 10
    Phase 1: Core 10
    Phase 2: Extended CoE Functions 11
    Prioritization and Execution 11

Part I: CS CoE Phase 1: Core 13

Chapter 2: CS Business and Operational Models 15

Common Business Models 16
    Models Based on Business Type 16
    Customer Success Models Based on Customer Tiers 19
    Customer Success Models Based on Company Maturity 22

TABLE OF CONTENTS

    The Five Pillars of Customer Success 28

    The Customer-Centric Business Model 36

    The Million-Dollar Question 37

Chapter 3: Key Customer Success Workflows and Processes 39

    Common Decision Points 40

    Key Processes 43

        Customer Journey Mapping 43

        Customer Onboarding 49

        Strategic Account Planning 51

    Customer Process Playbooks 55

        Optimizing Playbooks for Efficiency and Scale 59

    The Importance of Templatizing Workflows 65

    CSM Responsibility Models 66

Chapter 4: Customer Onboarding – A Methodology 75

    Scaling Your Onboarding 77

    Dimensions of Onboarding Maturity 81

Chapter 5: Key Metrics and Beyond 87

    Metrics vs. KPIs 88

    Leading vs. Lagging Health/Churn Indicators 102

        Leading Indicators 103

        Process Performance Metrics 107

    Examples of Quantitative Metrics Based on Company or Customer
    Journey Stage 108

    Capturing Quantitative Metrics 109

    Thinking Beyond Numbers – Co-defining Outcomes and KPIs 111

        Back to the Basics 111

        Co-defining Customer KPIs 112

TABLE OF CONTENTS

Outcomes-Driven Qualitative Metrics 113
    Capturing Qualitative Metrics 115
    Customer Perceived Value (CPV) 117

Chapter 6: Making Sense of Data 123

What Are Your Desired Outcomes? 125
How to Map Metrics to Desired Outcomes 126
Building a Customer 360 Dashboard 127
    Customer Health Indicators 129
    Company-wide KPIs 129
    Customer Success KPIs 130
Key Features of a Customer Success 360 Tool 132
Sample Dashboards 137
    Executive Dashboards 137
    Manager Dashboards 138
    CSM Dashboards 140
    Forecasting Dashboards 144

Chapter 7: Designing Customer Success for Scale 147

How to Build Customer Success for Scale 150
    Digital-Driven Customer Success Model 151
CS Data Modeling for Standardization 158
    Customer Data Model 158
    Action Plan for Building a Standardized Customer Data Model 160
Picking the Right Tools 166
Digital-Driven Process Automations 170
    Which Processes Are Candidates for Automating? 170
    How to Automate? 173
    Automation Examples 177

vii

TABLE OF CONTENTS

Chapter 8: Role of CS Operations in Scaling a CS Practice 183
What Is a Customer Success Operations Function? 184
What Is the Value of a CS Operations/CS CoE Function to a CS Org? 185
How Can a Dedicated CS Ops CoE Help Scale a CS Practice? 187
What Can Happen if a CS Team Tries to Scale Without Investing in CS Ops? 190
What Are the Blockers That Can Prevent CS Ops from Maximizing ROI from Their Role? 191
How to Maximize the Impact of CS Ops/CoE in an Organization? 191
Key Projects That Can Be Driven by CS Ops/CoE Team 192
Structure of a CS Operations/CoE Organization 192
Where Should the CS Operations Team Roll Up To? 192
Structure and Roles 193
CS Operations Team Roles 194
CS Operations Career Trajectory 196
CS Operations Resourcing 196
CS Operations Job Descriptions Examples 197
CS Team Velocity in Relation to CS Operations 205

Part II: CS CoE Phase 2: Extended Functions 209

Chapter 9: Extending CS CoE 211
CS Learning and Enablement 212
Role of CS CoE 213
CS L&E Metrics 213
CS Community Management 214
Partner Operations and Success Management 217

TABLE OF CONTENTS

Chapter 10: Where Are We Headed? 219
- Emerging Business Models 220
- Customer-Led Growth Model 221
- The New Era of Organic Growth and Creating Lifelong Customers 223
- Customer Success Predictions for a "New" World 225
- The Evolution of the Chief Customer Officer (CCO) Role 230
  - Is the CCO Role in Conflict with a Chief Sales Officer? 231
  - From CCO to CEO 232
- Role of Customer Success in Company Boards 232
- How You Should Prepare 235

Appendix A: The Evolution of Customer Success 237

Appendix B: Customer Account Team Roles and Responsibilities 243

Appendix C: Customer Satisfaction Survey Template 247

Glossary 251

References 255

Index 257

ix

About the Authors

Chitra Madhwacharyula is a seasoned Customer and Partner Success Leader with a proven track record of success in leading customer and partner engagement strategy, technical advisory, onboarding, adoption, retention, service monetization, and cross-functional teams to achieve exceptional business outcomes. With 20 years of global professional experience and a unique blend of innovative thinking and execution skills, Chitra brings a wealth of knowledge and expertise across a range of industries including hi-tech, finance, insurance, retail, manufacturing, and healthcare.

Chitra has worked with renowned companies such as Motorola, TIBCO, LinkedIn, Ayla Networks, Joveo, Couchbase, and HPE, where her focus was on building, delivering, standardizing and scaling Customer and Partner engagement practices and operations.

Chitra holds a Master's degree in Computer Science from the National University of Singapore and a Master's in Information Management from the University of California at Berkeley.

Shreesha Ramdas is a serial entrepreneur and a successful investor. Shreesha most recently was SVP & GM at Medallia. Previously, Shreesha was the CEO of Strikedeck, a leader in Customer Success Automation acquired by Medallia. Shreesha also was the co-founder of LeadFormix, a marketing automation platform that was acquired by Callidus/SAP. Shreesha also is an active investor/advisor in several growth companies including Workato, Boostup, Promethium, Tevent, Aavenier, Revv, Hirefly, Rocketlane, Narrato, Protecto, Empinfo, Opsera, Fullcast and several others.

Acknowledgments

We offer our sincerest thanks to all the industry leaders and practitioners who graciously shared their time and expertise. Their invaluable contributions have enriched the content, use cases, and examples in this book, making it more authentic and impactful.

We also want to extend our deepest appreciation to our families for their unwavering support during this multi-year writing journey. Without their help, this book would not have been possible.

To all of you, we express our heartfelt gratitude. Thank you!

Foreword

In 2015, Shreesha and I launched our respective Customer Success (CS) platform startups – Strikedeck and ChurnZero. We had similar philosophies on the Customer Success function, its value, market needs, and growth potential. So it was no surprise that we became competitors.

It wasn't until 2018 that we met in person during a panel discussion in Portland, Oregon. Initial light posturing on both sides transformed into a deep engaging conversation during which it became clear that we would become fast friends. As serial entrepreneurs, we still compete but our mutual respect, our common views on how to build a company, and our passion for Customer Success always come first.

Shreesha introduced me to Chitra. Her insights and experience growing companies and Customer Success teams make her a perfect co-author for writing a book about how organizations can prepare their CS practices for the next phase of Customer Success: standardization and scale.

The Customer Success industry is still new. As Shreesha and Chitra note, it has evolved from a break-fix/reactive customer engagement model to a proactive/strategic approach. But there is a lot of room to learn, grow, and expand. As the industry evolved, several books have been written about how to build a Customer Success function with a focus on Customer Success methodologies, philosophies, and best practices. However, as Shreesha and Chitra point out, we are now in the growth phase of Customer Success: CS 3.0. This is a phase where standardization and scale are required to cost-effectively amplify the value and reach of Customer Success.

FOREWORD

In a recent Customer Success leadership study, the definitive research report about the state of the industry, we saw that more than 82% of CS leaders have been in the industry less than ten years, and 44% less than five years. The good news is that more than 78% of CS leaders report to the C-suite, indicating that organizations have started appreciating the importance of the CS function. Many of these CS leaders have revenue responsibilities as well. Hence, as the CS function grows, it is critical to operationalize and scale it effectively.

Instinctively, Customer Success leaders and their CEOs know why they need to invest in improving Customer Success practices. But there is a lack of consensus on how to do it right. That is, until this book.

I value the practical in almost everything. This book appeals to me as it provides a comprehensive guide for scaling Customer Success. It details the key operational decision points and how to navigate them, and offers blueprints for the processes, workflows, automations, and engagement models needed to achieve desired growth outcomes. It outlines how to capture and analyze the right metrics at each stage of operational maturity. Most importantly, Shreesha and Chitra, in collaboration with other industry leaders who have contributed to this book, provide a step-by-step methodology to bring everything together to build a solid, scalable Customer Success practice that will benefit your organization and your customers.

Scaling Customer Success should be on every CS leader's and practitioner's bookshelf. Thank you, Shreesha and Chitra, for sharing your expertise and authoring this important book at a key juncture in the Customer Success evolution.

—You Mon Tsang
CEO and Co-founder
ChurnZero

Introduction

Customer churn afflicts companies around the world, putting profits and growth at risk. But how and why does churn happen? To answer that question, imagine a software company with recurring revenue of over $100MM annually. Imagine that, back in 2020, it was a leading supplier of security software in North America, with more than 1,000+ customers. Let's also give it a name: SoftCorp.

SoftCorp had a strategy for Customer Success. Knowing that 80% of its annual recurring revenue came from the top 20% of its customers, it invested in building a Customer Success organization aiming to provide a "white glove" post-sales experience to these top customers. But in doing so, it largely ignored the experience of the remaining 80% of customers. The strategy did indeed help the company retain its top customers. But relying on a small subset of customers resulted in an increased revenue and growth risk. Ignoring the experience of a large subset of its customers risked SoftCorp's broader footprint, overall growth potential and retention. This sub-optimal experience started causing blowback to the company's reputation, with its own customers and in broader industry circles. The result was customer churn of more than 10% annually, most of which came from mid- to lower-tier customers.

SoftCorp may be fictional but this is exactly the challenge faced by real-world SaaS and XaaS (Everything as a Service) companies. Initially, SaaS promised a recurring revenue stream that was predictable and grew rapidly. Customer revenue growth was compounding and lengthy implementations would become a thing of the past, lowering both operational and capital expenditures for SaaS customers. The SaaS customer experience would see a much needed series of improvements with new version releases, bug fixes, and new platforms/apps deployed either automatically or with a simple push of a button.

INTRODUCTION

But…SaaS has a down side. Due to the ease of onboarding, implementation, and version upgrades it has never been easier for a customer to move from vendor to vendor. There are a myriad of reasons that customers churn; however the reason always boils down to one thing: choice. Customers who experience product quality issues, onboarding challenges, product limitations, poor customer experiences, and more have a choice and they will exercise it. Moving to a different provider or vendor is fast and far easier than it has been in the past. When customers choose to go with another vendor, the financial impact can be tremendous. Software providers' revenue streams become less predictable and the compounding growth is limited.

So what is the solution for companies wishing to grow and retain your customer base?

As a Customer Success leader or practitioner, you already know where the answer lies. Customer Success owes its existence to proactive focus on maximizing customer outcomes realization and experience. Most companies have now incorporated some flavor of Customer Success within their own set up, choosing from the many Customer Success tools and methodologies to maximize and measure metrics like Net Promoter Scores, Customer Health Scores, First Time to value, Net Revenue Retention, and Annual Recurring Revenue (ARR) growth.

As we step into the next phase of Customer Success, it becomes important to start thinking about how to effectively scale this important function. It means going from offering a taste of Customer Success to just your top customers, to offering it to all your customers, irrespective of their tier, spend and current growth potential.

We call this latest evolution, Customer Success 3.0 (CS 3.0). CS 3.0 is a fundamental shift from product-centric to customer-centric and customer-led growth models with emphasis on standardization and scale. It involves converting the CS philosophies, ideas and best practices to usable operational models and building a Customer Success Center of Excellence (CS CoE) focused on standardizing, scaling and expanding Customer Success practices and methodologies to optimize customer and company success and ROI.

If you want to know more about the evolution of the Customer Success function, it is covered in the Appendix.

In this book, we introduce the Customer Success Center for Excellence (CS CoE) and its foundational principles, providing a practical guide for operationalizing your Customer Success practice. It delves into key questions such as; what operational processes and workflows need to be put in place based on the stage of your company, products, customer engagement models and desired outcomes, what are the crucial metri to measure and how can you capture them, what kinds of workflows do you need to implement, how do you map and analyze results and most importantly, scale your Customer Success practice effectively.

You can use this book as both a guide and a manual. Use it as a guide to become familiar with common Customer Success terminologies, concepts, workflows, metrics and their usage. Learn about the mission, goals and value of scaling a Customer Success practice by building a CS CoE organization. Use this book as a manual to operationalize your own Customer Success practice to maximize value, scale and effectiveness. Learn from Customer Success thought leaders on how they are building and operationalizing their own Customer Success practices.

AUTHOR'S BACKGROUND AND ORIGIN OF BOOK

Our own journey into customer engagement roles and Customer Success started in the 1990s. Collectively we have 40+ years of experience in building and growing companies and Customer Success organizations from scratch encompassing a variety of functions like product development, account management, business and technical consulting, professional services and support.

INTRODUCTION

We have worked closely with customers in industries like Hi-tech. Finance, Insurance, HR-tech, Gaming, Retail etc. in companies of different sizes including startups as we helped drive the evolution of Customer Success from a break-fix model focused on churn reduction (CS 1.0) to a proactive concierge white glove model for top customers (CS 2.0) and beyond. After a while, we started to realize that experienced Customer Success leaders and practitioners like ourselves were grappling with the same problems and ideas of how to standardize and scale CS beyond the top one or two tiers of customers and expand its footprint. After a lot of trial and error during our careers at multiple companies, we realized that we had the toolkit that could help CS leaders in companies around the world to evolve their CS practices to the next stage of CS (CS 3.0) that is driven by standardization, operationalization and automations of workflows and processes to maximize outcomes, scale, efficiencies, customer experience and growth.

And so the idea for this book was born, and thanks to feedback from numerous industry leaders and stakeholders, we have refined our experiences into the book you hold in your hands.

We hope that as you read this book, you will experience the same level of discovery and excitement that we went through along with culminating Aha! moments on creating method from madness. As Eleanor Roosevelt said, "Learn from the mistakes of others. You can't live long enough to make them all yourself."

CHAPTER 1

Customer Success Center of Excellence (CS CoE)

Enhancing and standardizing the customer experience for all customers is key to reducing churn and increasing the annual recurring revenue (ARR) and customer loyalty. But how can this be done? Let's return to SoftCorp, the fictional company we introduced in the Introduction. SoftCorp was fortunate to have a Chief Customer Officer (let's call her Janice) who understood that the company needed to expand its customer success footprint beyond its top tier customers in a cost-effective manner.

Janice believed she could do this by implementing a Customer Success Center of Excellence (CS CoE) within her Customer Success organization to standardize customer experience and deploy customer engagement best practices and processes at scale. This would help expand SoftCorp's Customer Success Org. footprint to all of their customers, maximizing adoption and customer outcomes across all customer tiers.

Janice was right. Less than two years later, profits were up and, more importantly, customers across the board were raving about the world-class experience offered by SoftCorp. Customer Success became a major differentiator for the company compared to its competitors.

CHAPTER 1   CUSTOMER SUCCESS CENTER OF EXCELLENCE (CS COE)

Our example makes it sound simple, but it goes without saying that there is much work to be done to set up a Customer Success Center of Excellence (hereon also referred to as CS CoE). Building a consistent, repeatable and reliable customer experience is so much more than a series of delivery motions driven by Customer Success or Delivery Managers.

In this chapter, we will examine the role of the CS CoE, discuss its core and specialized functions, and look at the phases involved in building one from scratch. By doing this, you can build a world-class, unified Customer Success practice across the entire company, allowing customers and partners to thrive in a "Anything as-a-service" (XaaS) environment.

The core mission of a CS CoE is to develop and execute a strategy to standardize and scale customer success methodologies and practices. This ensures an optimal, predictable customer experience leading to maximal desired outcomes, adoption retention, and growth. Ideally, this is done by setting up the right listening posts to capture the right data, using that data to deploy standard CS methodologies and playbooks and triggering timely actions based on key leading indicators to optimize adoption and customer experience and/or mitigate risk and churn.

Customer Success is much more than a function within a company focused on maximizing customers' desired outcomes, experience, and growth. It is a mindset that needs to exist, top down and across the board, with all company stakeholders bought into making their customers successful and understanding what it involves. Hence building a successful CS CoE requires buy-in and investment from the company leadership team and a strong partnership with cross-functional stakeholders and key partners, not just strategically but also operationally to be able to put the right methodologies and resources in place and ensure that they are embraced and adopted cross-functionally as applicable.

It is also ideal if post-sales/(or as some companies call it, post-win) customer-facing departments work from the same playbook with handoffs clearly defined. At a minimum, Customer Success, Professional Services, and other Delivery teams should be aligned on their operational processes to offer a seamless customer experience. The CS CoE needs to ensure that there are shared processes, customer data, and a common set of standards and metrics to facilitate interlocks among cross-functional and/or geographically distributed teams.

As you can see, there could be significant groundwork to establish the CS CoE. But don't let that deter you. The goal should be to start small with the CS CoE core functions and a limited set of key customer engagement workflows and playbooks that you want to standardize. Once you have successfully piloted those and shown impact, you can expand the proven approach more broadly to other processes, teams, and geographies.

Customer Success CoE Functions

The components for building a CS CoE are shown in Figure 1-1. CS Workflows and Process Management, Tools and Systems Management, Portfolio and Resource Management, and Analytics are some of the foundational functions to build a CS CoE and usually clubbed together as CS Operations. CS Learning and Enablement, Community Management, Partnership Operations are additional functions that can fall within the CS CoE scope of responsibilities as it matures. A digital engagement strategy should span across all these areas to build a scalable CS operational model from get go.

CHAPTER 1 CUSTOMER SUCCESS CENTER OF EXCELLENCE (CS COE)

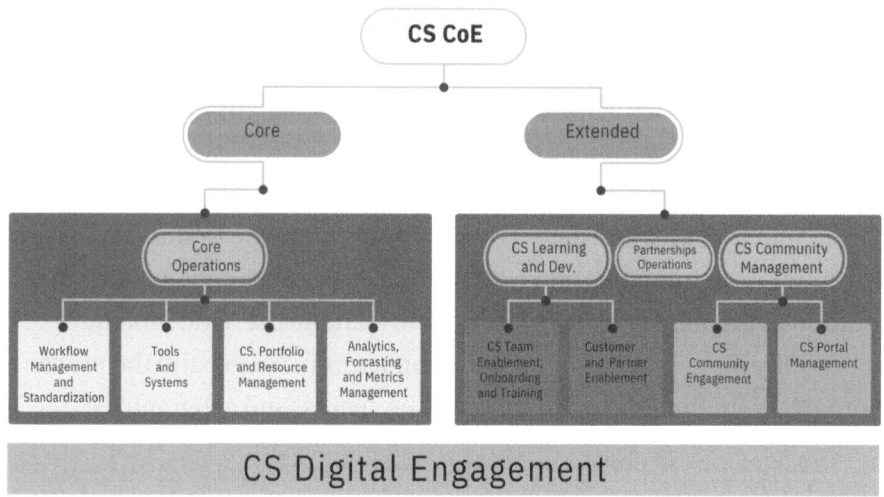

Figure 1-1. *The components of a CS CoE*

Let us now look at these functions in more detail, starting with the core functions and moving on to the extended functions that are typically found in larger mature CS CoEs.

Core Functions

CS Operations Management, commonly known as CS Ops, is gaining traction as a key supporting function for a Customer Success organization. The goal of CS Ops. is to manage, scale, and monitor all CS operations for maximum efficiency and effectiveness. It is similar to the SalesOps function that supports the Sales team.

The scope of CS Ops can encompass responsibilities like the standardization and management of CS workflows and processes such as customer journey maps and playbooks, management of CS tools and systems tech stack, creation of dashboards and reports to track key metrics, management of CS team members' customer portfolio assignments, CS forecasting, predictive analytics, and digital automations (Tech-Touch).

The CS Tools and Systems team is responsible for selecting the right technology stack for the global customer success teams and deploying and maintaining it across the enterprise globally. They are also responsible for deploying the playbooks defined by the Workflows team properly in the tools for seamless adoption. We will expand further on the different options for a CS tech stack in later chapters.

The CS Analytics team is responsible for creating and managing CS dashboards and reports with a goal of tracking key metrics like the customers and customer success practice's health and enabling accurate and data-driven forecasting and risk management.

These are the core functions of every CS CoE. If your company is a late-stage startup with more than 100 customers or bigger, and/or if you have significant CS Learning and Enablement and Partnership needs, you will probably want to expand its remit.

Extended Functions
CS Learning and Enablement (L&E)

The CS Learning and Enablement function's primary goal is to make sure that Customer Success team members like Customer Success Managers (CSMs) and Architects (CSAs) are fully skilled and enabled to become trusted advisors and effective product and strategy consultants to customers. Its scope of responsibilities includes creation and delivery of business process documentation, guides, and best practices. It also drives the Customer Success team's training curriculum and delivery.

The L&E team onboards new CS team members and builds and delivers upskilling and ongoing trainings and certifications to keep the customer facing CS teams up-to-date on their company products and features, industry standards, CS methodologies and tools, best practices, forecasting management, etc.

If your company has a partner ecosystem (channel partners, delivery partners, etc.), the CS L&E team can also onboard and enable Partner CSMs along with internal CS team members.

In addition to these responsibilities, if your company does not have a separate external-facing customer education team, this team can take on the broader responsibility of creating and delivering training and certification content for your customers, your partners' customers, and broader user community members as well. Within this expanded scope, this team develops and executes the strategy for customer training programs to achieve an empathetic and memorable experience for every customer.

The material and processes created by the CS Learning and Enablement team can also be leveraged by the CS Community Management team that manages the broader user community of your products.

CS Community Engagement and Management

The Customer Success Community Engagement and Management function focuses on building and growing a healthy community of product users, advocates, and contributors through community-based initiatives like user and partner forums, user meetups and conferences, focus groups, and workshops. This team can leverage the learning management tools and workflows built by the CS Learning and Development team to educate and enable the broader community of users. The goal of this team is to expand your company's user ecosystem and create champions and advocates of your company and its offerings. Some of the initiatives managed by this team can be joint cross functional initiatives with the Marketing, Sales and other teams.

This team is especially important when you have open-source versions of your products which are not supported by your CS and Support teams and/or if you have a cross-section of your customers that are not actively supported by Customer Success.

In companies that have big, distributed Customer Success teams with hundreds of CSMs, the CS Community Engagement team can also, or in some cases primarily, focus on internal CS community management. They ensure that the global CS community feels connected with the centralized CS CoE Org by evangelizing and communicating the processes rolled out by CS CoE in the right way. This helps maximize receptivity, change management, and adoption. Activities driven by this team can include sending regular newsletters, conducting global team meetings, webinars, and internal CS Community events, managing CS community chat rooms and portals, identifying and celebrating CS champions, and helping propagate the CS mindset throughout the company.

If a CS CoE is going to be effective in defining and implementing a standardized customer experience through operational excellence, then it is important that it extends that experience to your channel partners' customers. This ensures that the partners' customers who use your company's products are offered a similar and consistent experience as your direct customers. This can be managed by the Partnerships Operations function.

Partnerships Operations

Many CS Organizations also manage the operations of their partners through their Partner Success Managers. A Partner Success Manager typically works with one or more existing partners of a company to make sure they offer a consistent experience to their end customers that's similar to that of the company's direct customers.

A CS CoE can provide guidance to help define the partner's own Customer Success setup and customer engagement workflows to be consistent with your company's customer engagement workflows. This ensures that your company's customers get a consistent experience irrespective of whether they purchase your products and/or services directly from your company or through a partner.

Managing partner operations can include tasks like assisting partners with building their own Customer Success and Support practices, managing portfolio assignments of Partner Success Managers and monitoring partners' health by tracking key metrics. Many of your own Customer Success team's workflows, metrics, and dashboards should be able to be repurposed to manage partner operations as well, although there might be a need for some customization and augmentation to factor in specific partnership nuances, requirements, and packaging of your offerings for partners. It is key that your CS Partner Operations team works closely with the broader Partner Business Development team, similar to how your regular CS team works with your Sales team, to identify the handoffs, R&R, and scope of responsibilities.

As discussed earlier, a key outcome for CS CoE is to scale CS processes cost-effectively across all customer tiers and selected partners. Doing this requires a well-thought-out digital engagement strategy that minimizes the use of manual resources, manages risk and experience, and drives automated or semi-automated customer retention and expansion plays.

CS Digital Engagement Strategy

An optimal digital engagement strategy enables Customer Success teams to optimize customers' experience through the use of technology. This is a key scaling initiative for Customer Success teams and CS CoEs for both core and extended functions with an aim to maximize digital engagement and expand tech touch enabled Customer Success to all customers irrespective of their tier or segmentation. It also helps enhance customers' experience by leveraging automations and self-serve technology.

Examples of digital-driven customer engagement include triggering automated onboarding emails to customers to welcome them and give them a simple checklist to start their onboarding process, automating processes like Support setup and CSM assignment based on the stage of the Sales cycle, and automated flagging of issues like low adoption.

Digital CS Engagement does not equate to just tech touch and/or self-serve and is not limited to mid- and low-tier customers. Instead, it's an engagement strategy that can be applied to customers of any size. Defining a holistic digital engagement strategy and executing it by leveraging the CS Ops, Tooling, Learning and Enablement, and Community functions is vital for building a strong CS CoE and hence, by extension, a strong CS practice.

Now that we understand all the major components of a CS CoE, let us delve deeper into how to practically build a strong foundation for it.

How to Build a CS CoE Organization

In this book, we will focus primarily on the core CS operational management (CS Ops) functions like Workflows and Processes, Tooling and Systems, Analytics and Digital Engagement since they are the key foundation stones for a strong CS CoE.

While it is perfectly fine to have your CS CoE focus primarily on your core operational functions at the beginning, some companies may want to include other functions like CS L&E from the get-go. That should be fine. What we are proposing here is a Minimum Viable Product (MVP) for building a CS CoE.

Based on your needs, you can include one or more of the extended functions in your original CS CoE scope if you have the strategy and resources to support them. Or you can extend your CS CoE as needed once your core functions and teams are set up. How quickly this will happen will depend on your CS CoE investment, priority, and maturity of your CS processes and playbooks. You could be looking at 6–12 months to build a CS CoE from scratch depending on your MVP use cases, number of customers, complexity of workflows, and how much groundwork you have already done for standardizing your CS processes and workflows.

CHAPTER 1   CUSTOMER SUCCESS CENTER OF EXCELLENCE (CS COE)

From Theory to Practice
Phase 1: Core

So if you want to build a CS CoE, how and where do you begin? In the rest of this book, we'll give you step-by-step guidance on how to envision and design the foundational components for your CS CoE. We will primarily focus on how to build your CS operations functions based on your company stage, product stage, and CS maturity model. The overarching goal is to build and support a CS practice that is ready for scale and optimized for efficiency. Such a CS CoE is primed and ready to evolve and expand along with your overall CS practice as you take your company to the next levels of CS maturity.

As explained in the CS Maturity Evolution section in the Appendix, the three stages of CS evolution are CS 1.0: Reactive → CS 2.0 Proactive → CS 3.0 Scale. CS 3.0 is focused on standardizing and scaling the CS practice by defining standard workflows, deploying them in the right tools, and leveraging digital-led automations to optimize and scale. CS CoE is the umbrella under which the CS 3.0 ecosystem is built and executed.

The six stages of building the CS CoE Core functions are shown in Figure 1-2. From mapping the right business model for your CS practice to implementing the right workflows and playbooks to measuring the right metrics and finally scaling your CS practice to all your customers; this can be a blueprint for setting up your CS CoE, which you can customize based on your own unique needs. We have organized this book to align with this blueprint and follow the same flow.

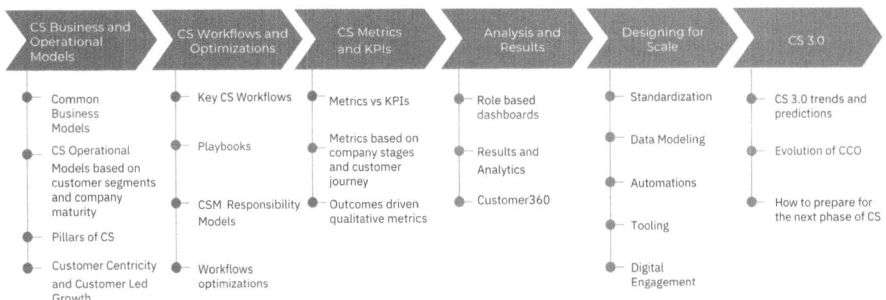

Figure 1-2. Steps to build the core components of a CS CoE

Phase 2: Extended CoE Functions

Once the foundational components for a CS practice and operations are in place, the CS CoE can be extended to include functions like CS Learning and Enablement, CS Community Management, Partnership Operations, etc. We won't explore these functions in detail in this book since we will be focused on how to build and optimize the CS CoE's essential core.

Prioritization and Execution

As you build out your CS CoE, it is important to assess your organization's current maturity, business model, product, customers, Customer Success maturity, and priorities. At its most basic and to begin with, your CS CoE could be one or a small team of CS operatives, who help manage existing CS workflows and tools and create metrics-driven dashboards/reports. At its most sophisticated, it will be a global, holistic CS CoE function that is built on a solid foundation of repurposable and standardized workflows, toolsets, and specialized sub-functions servicing multiple geographies, products, customer and partner tiers, and broader user community. The global, holistic CS CoE defines, manages, and analyzes all post-sales customer experiences, touchpoints, and engagements.

CHAPTER 1   CUSTOMER SUCCESS CENTER OF EXCELLENCE (CS COE)

Whether big or small, you should envision and lay out the building blocks of your CS practice and CS CoE very carefully so they can be easily extended and expanded for scale and efficiency to avoid costly re-orgs and rework. In this book, we will provide the key principles and guidelines you need to keep in mind as you start building your Customer Success Center of Excellence.

In the next chapter, we'll look at some common and upcoming business and operational models based on company size, CS maturity, and other parameters based on which you can model your own CS practice and CoE organization.

PART I

CS CoE Phase 1: Core

CHAPTER 2

CS Business and Operational Models

Where does Customer Success fit into an organization? Back in 2010, one of us was speaking at a conference when one of the audience asked a perceptive question at the end of the talk. She asked: "Where should Customer Success roll up to?" It was a good question and one that her company, a $100MM+ provider of security software, had grappled with. We've seen firsthand how different companies tackled it in different ways. In some, Customer Success reported directly to the CEO or CRO, but that wasn't universal. In our own experience, we have seen Customer Success to also roll upto Support, Marketing, Sales, and, in some cases even to Product.

So what is the optimum setup? We'll come back to this question, but first we'll review some common and upcoming business and operational models and explore how Customer Success methodologies can be adapted for them. We will also cover the concepts of CS 3.0 and the five pillars of Customer Success. Think of this chapter as laying the knowledge foundation for your CS practice. In order to build your CS CoE, you need to have a good understanding of the business and operational models of your current CS practice. This will enable you to not only effectively standardize and operationalize your current CS practice but also plan for its evolution. It is also a good idea to correlate the information in this chapter with your own Customer Success practice.

Common Business Models
Models Based on Business Type
Software as a Service (Plug n Play)

Customer Success, as a practice, was introduced primarily for SaaS B2B business models as a mechanism to prevent churn. We will look at variations of SaaS business models in this section, starting with the simple plug n play business model with reduced barriers to entry and exit. Netflix, Door Dash, Uber, and other consumer-focused products and companies are examples of this model.

In the SaaS plug n play B2C business model, a Customer Success Organization does not typically exist to support the customers directly. Customer Success Orgs. are typically introduced in these companies to manage partners and to manage B2B customers if they exist.

Although a traditional Customer Success Org. may not exist in these companies, many of them invest in a Customer Success operational model to support quick, easy, and automated onboarding and fast time to value for their end customers. Sometimes, especially in monthly subscription models with easy cancellation policies, churn could happen at any time and without notice. So Customer Success operational models in these companies focus on data-driven metrics to monitor usage, adoption, and customer experience.

They constantly have to make sure that the customer adoption does not flag since that would be a serious leading churn indicator. The significant subscriber churn that Netflix experienced during the COVID-19 pandemic is a perfect example of the low barriers of entry and exit and the risks of this business model.

Platform/Infrastructure as a Service (PaaS/IaaS)

SaaS has now evolved into variants like B2B PaaS (Platform as a Service) and IaaS (Infrastructure as a Service) and XaaS (Everything as a Service). Cloud-based B2B companies like AWS, Google, Salesforce, Oracle and many others are examples of these business models.

The basic business model could still be consumption-based subscription, but the level of engagement with customers in these models is more involved than the typical plug n play SaaS. That's because the barriers of entry and exit could be more complex, and in some cases, could also involve hardware deployments.

For example, Salesforce provides a highly customizable customer relationship management platform and AWS provides the cloud infrastructure for companies to build and deploy their own products. If your company has a similar platform offering, it takes considerable investment and resources from your customers to develop, deploy, and configure their products and processes on your platform. So once your customers have invested in your platform, they cannot easily switch to a competitor without some lead time. Their current batch of products are locked in to use your platform/infrastructure because of the unique setup and hardware requirements that come with it.

For example, if you've deployed your products on AWS and after a while, you want to switch to Google Cloud Platform (GCP) instead, it will not happen at the flip of a switch and will require some transition time due to the planning and investment needed to move your products from AWS to GCP. In this model, the time to value for the customer is typically longer than simple plug n play because it needs some configuration and/or development of products.

CHAPTER 2   CS BUSINESS AND OPERATIONAL MODELS

Traditional Non-SaaS/on-Prem and Evolution to XaaS

In traditional on-prem business models, customers purchase your company's products to be used on their own premises with no shared platform or infrastructure environment or consumption-based billing setup.

A common example of this model is hardware and/or manufacturing companies that sell products that are physically shipped to customers to be installed or deployed. Hence, workflows related to supply chain, logistics, and installation will become part of the customer's experience and need to be factored into your Customer Success operational model.

For example, in B2B hardware businesses like HPE or Intel, where hardware products like servers or computer chips are shipped to customers, the CS operational approach could be similar to the PaaS/IaaS operational models. Differences could include non-consumption-based pricing and additional workflows to factor in shipping, supply chain, and logistics.

Some companies like HPE are transforming to a XaaS consumption-based model despite requirement to ship and set up hardware on prem. This hybrid XaaS model could have some unique workflows based on supply chain, logistics, H/W setup, site reviews requirements that need to be factored into the customer experience workflows and CS CoE methodologies. Irrespective of your business model, the focus on the following should stay consistent to ensure long-term customer retention and minimize customer churn:

- Fast time to value
- Good customer experience
- Maximizing customer ROI
- Promoting strategic growth

CHAPTER 2   CS BUSINESS AND OPERATIONAL MODELS

Once you have a good understanding of your core business model, the next step is to understand the different CS Operational models based on customer tiers.

Customer Success Models Based on Customer Tiers

Figure 2-1 shows an example of a Customer Success model based on customer segmentation that we built at one of our companies. Many companies classify their customer tiers as Strategic, Enterprise, and Others. A High Touch CS model is mapped to strategic customers, a Mid Touch model is mapped to enterprise customers, and a Digital/Tech Touch model mapped to the rest. For many companies, partners' success setup could also have such a classification and could require a similar tiered operational model. Let us now look at the different customer tiers and the associated customer success operational models.

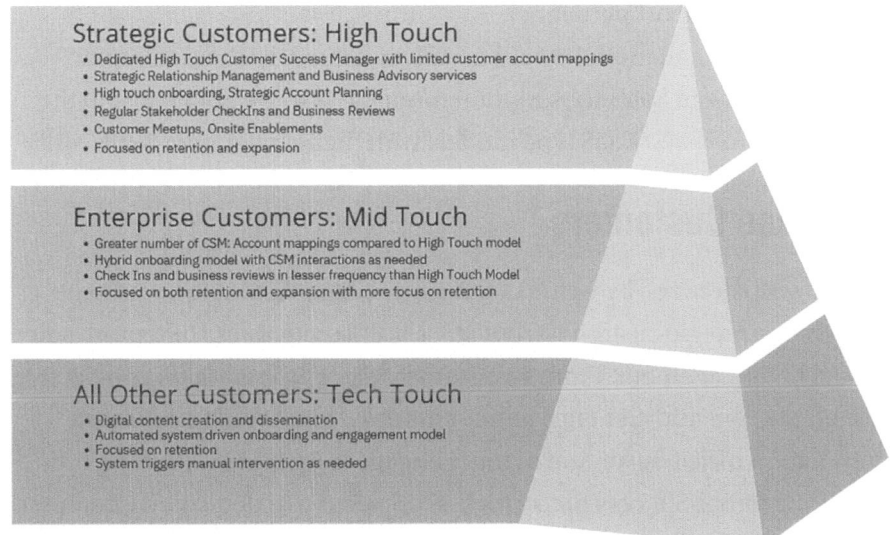

Figure 2-1. Customer Success models based on customer tiers

19

CHAPTER 2   CS BUSINESS AND OPERATIONAL MODELS

Strategic Customers

Strategic customers are defined as customers that meet a defined threshold of spend (ARR/NRR) and/or are classified as high growth/key accounts that will maintain (if sufficiently high) and ideally exceed the threshold of spend in a defined time frame. They usually form a small but significant subset of a company's total customers and are many times responsible for a significant portion (20–80%+) of the company's recurring revenue.

From an operational perspective, these customers require, and in many cases demand, high touch white glove treatment. This includes a dedicated post-sales account team with a designated high-touch Customer Success Manager (CSM). This dedicated CSM is a trusted advisor and business consultant who helps solidify and grow the customer relationship to a tight-knit partnership, as opposed to a traditional customer-vendor model. In many cases, depending on the requirements of onboarding and deployments, these customers also require dedicated professional services and customer support personnel.

This operational model would usually not apply to the traditional quick-in, quick-out SaaS subscription model. It is more applicable to the sticky B2B PaaS/IaaS/XaaS type models with higher customer NRR/ARR.

Enterprise Customers

Enterprise customers, by virtue of their associated NRR/ARR, would be lower than strategic customers, but still significant enough to require some manual CS engagement. From a Customer Success operations perspective, they fall into the mid-tier engagement model. They could be offered a combination of self-serve and manual engagement and be serviced by a pool of Customer Success personnel, as opposed to a dedicated Customer Success manager for every account.

All Other customers

The third, often neglected, tier is the long tail that does not meet the spend and/or growth criteria of strategic and enterprise customers. Many times, these customers are offered little or no Customer Success exposure and engagement and have to rely on themselves and their Sales account team to derive value from their investment. That, however, is the wrong approach. As companies are becoming more mature in their Customer Success operations, they are realizing that it is important to offer a good experience to all customers, irrespective of their tier.

It is important to track the health and adoption of every customer in order to maintain a critical mass of adoption and grow market penetration, have a handle on customer health and adoption across all customer tiers and identify underdeveloped and underutilized customer accounts and tap their growth potential.

Today's low spenders could evolve to enterprise and strategic accounts if given the right attention and support. By volume, a large number of low-spending accounts could be as key to a company's revenue as a small number of high-spenders. It would therefore be a mistake to completely ignore this tier.

While it is not practical or financially viable to offer all customers the same level of post-win engagement as strategic and enterprise customers, it is still beneficial for all customers to have access to a Customer Success experience focused on maximizing their outcomes and experience via the digital tech touch operational model.

The digital tech touch model focuses on building and deploying self-serve and automated tools at scale for onboarding, ongoing support, enablement, and monitoring the health and activity of customers. This CS sub function is really the foundation of CS 3.0 that targets standardization, scale, and optimization. The digital/tech touch operational model is not limited to the long tail customers. If deployed correctly, it can be a valuable tool for strategic and enterprise customers as well to help improve their overall engagement experience. We will explore this model more in future chapters.

CHAPTER 2 CS BUSINESS AND OPERATIONAL MODELS

Now that we have looked at the different CS operational models based on business type and customer segmentation, let's look at customer success operational models based on company maturity.

Customer Success Models Based on Company Maturity

Your Customer Success maturity model will be driven by your company maturity and your customer profiles, as shown in Figure 2-2.

Figure 2-2. *Business maturity mapping to desired customer types*

Once you've identified the maturity of your business, you can find appropriate focus areas and execution recommendations/tactics for consideration, as laid out in Table 2-1.

CHAPTER 2 CS BUSINESS AND OPERATIONAL MODELS

Table 2-1. *Customer Success Focus Areas Based on Company Maturity*

Company maturity	Focus	Key objective	Tactics
Early-stage startup (<10MM ARR)	Advocacy	Adoption	• Build customer personas, journey maps • Initiate thinking on segmentation • Begin defining playbooks • Overinvest in the care of customers
Mid-stage startup (10-50MM ARR)	Process	Retention	Everything in previous section + • Operationalize processes • Do segmentation and playbooks mapping • Define and execute metrics • Formalize advocacy and upsell programs
Late-stage startups and enterprises (> 50MM)	Scaling	Advocacy at scale	Everything in previous section + • Manage user community, annual conferences, local events • Create specialized teams – onboarding, adoption, training (university) • Define and operationalize benchmarks • Create customer reference program • Manage Customer Advisory Board execution

23

CHAPTER 2 CS BUSINESS AND OPERATIONAL MODELS

Early-Stage Startup

If you are an early-stage startup, a fundamental question is whether you even need a Customer Success function. Traditionally, many companies focused 100% of their investments on Sales and Product functions. Customer Success usually did not make an appearance till the later stages of the company. This model has been steadily changing, especially in the hi-tech sector, where more and more startups are realizing that it is not enough for them simply to acquire customers.

What helps a startup evolve to a mature and successful company faster is its ability to retain early customers and grow them many times over. Often, customer acquisition of initial customers happens fairly easily, based on the pre-existing relationships of startup founders or investors. Usually, these customers (even if they are big brand names) start small with minimal initial Total Contract Values (TCV) to try things out because of the inherent risks in deploying an unknown product or solution from a relatively unknown company. The real challenge, once they are won, is to convert them into long-term customers by exhibiting ongoing, consistent value and ROI. Hence Customer Success.

The focus of CS in these early-stage companies is on customers' time to value, adoption, retention, and overall satisfaction. The scope of CS responsibility can be fairly broad. It can include all post-sales/post-win management and delivery functions so the sales team can focus exclusively on acquiring new leads and closing new logos. Customer Success becomes the conduit between the customer, company execs, and product/engineering teams.

The Customer Success Managers (CSMs) also play the key role of a business consultant to identify and bridge the gap between the company's products and customers' needs. This can be critical for customer retention and expansion. Startups can react faster than larger enterprises, with bug fixes and enhancements for the most important customers. A strong

CHAPTER 2 CS BUSINESS AND OPERATIONAL MODELS

CS function with a focus on business consulting can be a significant differentiator to create referenceable customers and champions.

The CSMs, for their portfolio accounts, play the role of a customer consultant and quarterback by having a handle on their customers' requirements and mapping them back to their own company's products and services to help drive customer priorities, experience, and satisfaction. They can also collect and transmit customers' feedback to the Product teams and assist with product gap analysis. This helps drive customer led growth, long-term customer loyalty and products roadmap by identifying the right priorities and pulling in the right resources to solidify the initial customer investment and relationship.

Figure 2-3 shows how such a CS Org. setup might look in practice. Let's imagine an early-stage startup, NewBiz, with 80 employees and 20MM ARR. It decides it needs a CS Org. to manage customer churn and experience. It hires a Head of CS, who hires the first few CSMs to focus exclusively on managing its top ten customers. The other customers are managed by the sales team. The CS team starts from zero, defining its customer playbooks and journey maps. Initially, it leverages existing tools it already has, like Salesforce, to build out the customer engagement process before moving to a full-fledged CS tool after a couple of years.

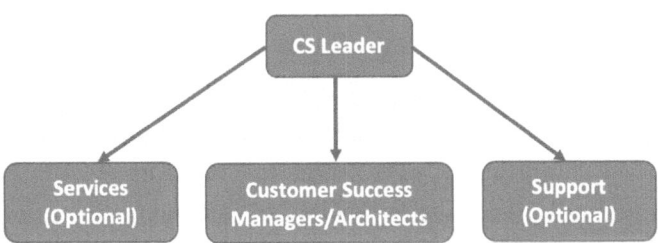

Figure 2-3. *Customer Success Org. structure in early-stage startups*

Mid-stage Startup

A mid-stage startup should have a Customer Success function that would fulfill the CS responsibilities outlined in the early-stage startup section. In addition, CS should have a longer-term focus on strategic engagement and expansion. Depending on the type of company and product complexity, CS could be responsible for NRR, expansion and/or product adoption, Customer Experience (CX), and Customer Satisfaction (CSAT).

This is also a good phase to start identifying the need and opportunities for packaged and monetized training and professional services offerings. Due diligence should be done to fully flush out the different phases of the customer journey, starting from pre-sales. This will help you understand and explore usage/adoption patterns, barriers to entry, leading churn indicators, gaps between customer needs and current product capabilities, and enablement barriers. All of this is done with a view to standardize and scale Customer Success.

Based on the findings of this discovery process, company leaders can decide the focus areas for short-, mid-, and long-term company and Customer Success strategy. This is also a good time to start investing in optimization and automation tools to enable cost and resource optimization and scale, with an eventual goal of a cost-neutral CS organization.

The CS team at this stage can consist of a multi-level CS hierarchical model with different sub-functions like Account Management, Services, Support, and Consulting with an overarching CS leader (VP or CCO) at the helm. There can also be a fledgling CS Ops/CoE function to support the CS Org that focuses on operational excellence and churn/growth forecasting based on leading indicators.

Figure 2-4 shows an example of a CS organization in a mid-stage PaaS company with 100+ employees and geographically distributed customers and teams managed by a central CS Org.

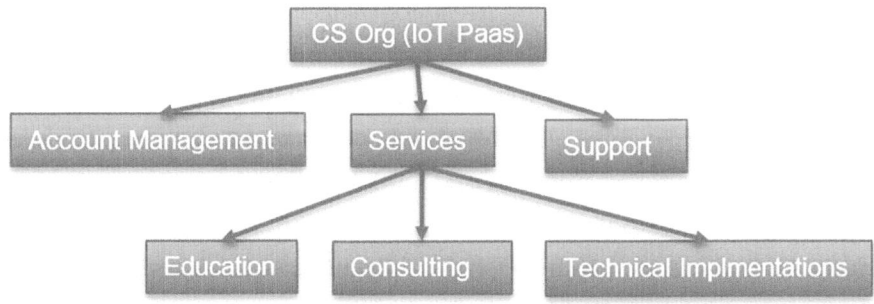

Figure 2-4. An example of a CS Org. structure in a mid-stage PaaS company

Late-Stage Startups and Enterprise

Enterprise companies can have expansive CS models segmented in different ways, such as based on customer type/tier/segment, industry, geography, etc., and also to span all customer tiers. They can also explore different strategies to flush out and consolidate Professional Services, Consulting, Technical Account Management, and so on as cost-neutral sub-functions within the Customer Success umbrella. Alternatively, they might choose to keep them as separate functions based on their original setup and evolution.

They also have opportunities to invest in an enterprise-wide standard post-sales/post-win operational models and tools with a customer-centric focus. By doing so, they can focus on expanding global strategic partnerships with high-end customers, while providing a Customer Success experience to other customers with a digital tech-touch approach.

From a team organization perspective, depending on the size of the company and setup, Customer Success teams could have regional leaders and hubs/pods supporting local customers and partners. These teams can potentially start taking on quota-carrying responsibilities at some point based on NRR, with accelerated models for growth and expansion.

An important decision point, irrespective of company maturity, is where Customer Success rolls up to. It is recommended that CS is a primary function that rolls up to the CEO/COO or CRO directly, since its goals and desired outcomes are sufficiently distinct and not influenced by the goals of a different function that it might roll up into. If a question arises as to whether CS is closest to Sales or Support, the answer is neither. CS is closest to Business Consulting and outcomes and value management.

Now let's look at the pillars of Customer Success and the role they play in building out a Customer Success Org. and CS CoE function.

The Five Pillars of Customer Success

Back in 2005, management consultancy Bain & Company interviewed companies and their customers. It wanted to find out if there was a gap between perceptions of the experience that companies feel they are providing to their customers, and customers' own perception of that experience. The results, as shown in Figure 2-5, showed that there was a gap – an astoundingly big one. It's the perfect example of why companies need to invest in a holistic customer success strategy and operational model. Furthermore, you need regular and active incorporation of customer data to measure the effectiveness of your models. A CS practice built on a strong foundation of data and standardization can help mitigate the risk identified by the Bain study.

CHAPTER 2 CS BUSINESS AND OPERATIONAL MODELS

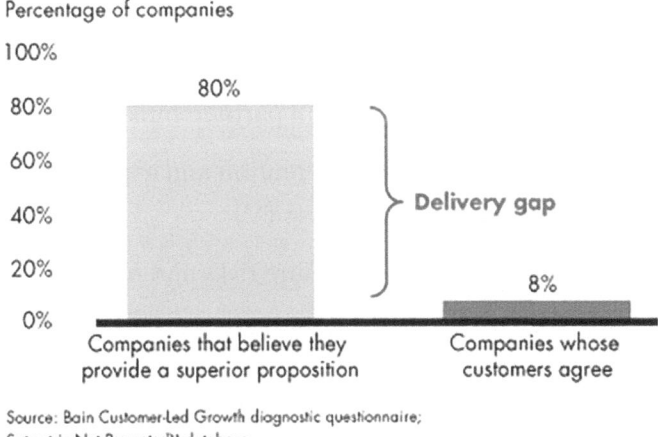

Figure 2-5. Bain and Company customer experience survey results

Irrespective of your Customer Success operational model and company maturity, there are five pillars of Customer Success that you need to incorporate in your overall CS Strategy, as shown in Figure 2-6.

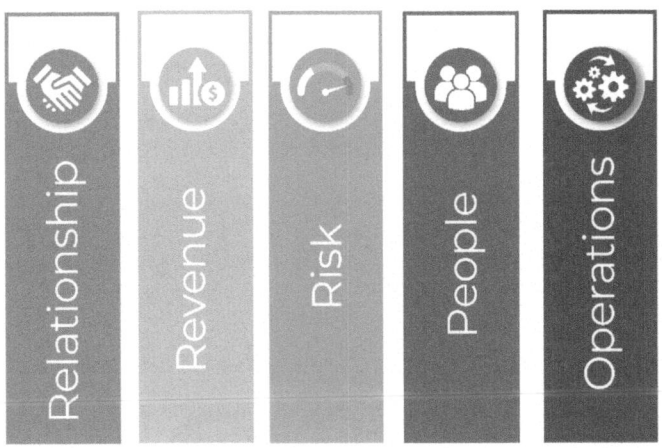

Figure 2-6. The Five Pillars of Customer Success

CHAPTER 2   CS BUSINESS AND OPERATIONAL MODELS

Here's how we define each of the five pillars:

- **Relationship:** How to strengthen customer relationships to form long-term partnerships
- **Revenue:** How to maximize retention and expansion and customer Life Time Value (LTV)
- **Risk:** How to proactively measure risks and mitigate
- **People:** How to introduce a culture of operational rigor and governance at scale
- **Data/Operations:** Which facets of the workflows to operationalize at scale, which dashboards to create, and which metrics to measure

The pillars relate to each other in the manner shown in Figure 2-7, while the different activities that are part of each pillar are shown in Figure 2-8.

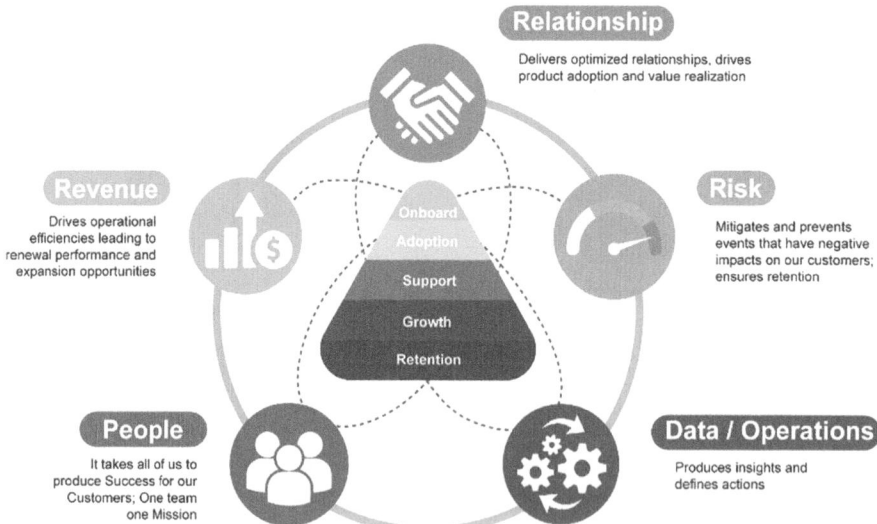

Figure 2-7. *The relationship between the pillars of Customer Success*

30

CHAPTER 2 CS BUSINESS AND OPERATIONAL MODELS

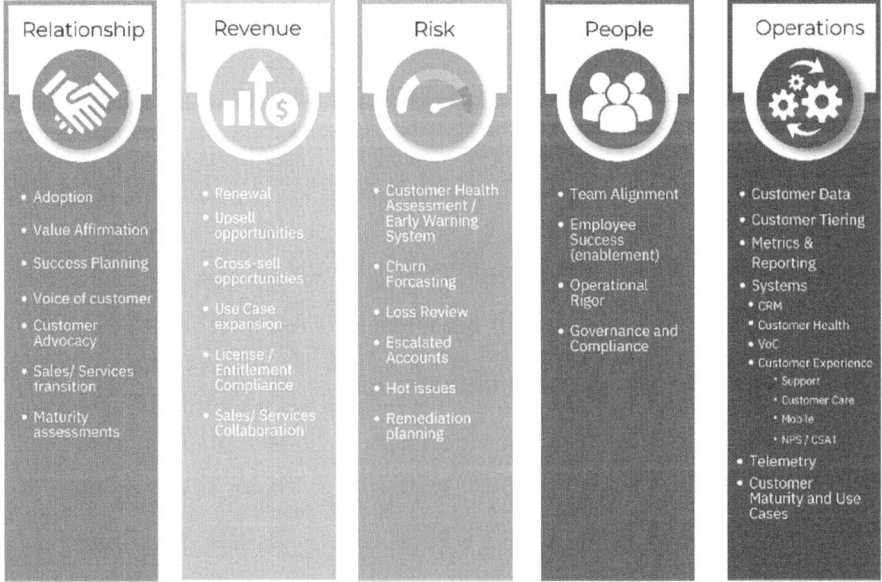

Figure 2-8. *Components of the Customer Success pillars*

It is important to keep the following decision points in mind when you are building your CS strategy:

1. Which playbooks and tasks apply to your current CS operational model with a focus on your customer journey and use cases

2. Which ones to prioritize and in what order

3. How do they correlate to achieve the desired outcomes

4. Which ones to park for future evolution and scaling

5. How to segment these tasks per customer tier, journey, partner, etc., based on:

    a. Relevance

CHAPTER 2   CS BUSINESS AND OPERATIONAL MODELS

    b. Applicability (are they applicable only for partners or certain customer tiers?)

    c. Tasks Distribution: who does what – internal resources, partners, customers, etc.

6. What artifacts to use

7. How to measure effectiveness of strategy

8. Whether to automate or not automate and how

9. What kinds of dashboards to create

You could build a custom operational model based on a phase of the customer journey or a specific use case, for example, for churn mitigation, as shown in Figure 2-9.

***Figure 2-9.** Example of churn mitigation*

Up to this point, we've looked at CS Operations in the context of broader company maturity models. Let us now flush out some of the focus areas within each Customer Success pillar based on company maturity (Table 2-2).

32

CHAPTER 2　CS BUSINESS AND OPERATIONAL MODELS

Table 2-2. Customer Success Pillars Focus Areas Based on Company Maturity

Stage	Relationship	Revenue	Risk	People	Operations
Startup	White glove treatment for all customers served by CS (big brands or significant ARR). Value affirmation is important. Building credibility and customer trust in product quality and company longevity is key	Renewal. Use case expansion. Customer champions	Customer loss to more established brands. Loss analysis. Keeping up with ongoing customer demand. High risk of churn. Escalations handling. Gaps review. Loss review.	Small Customer Success team with hands-on leader. Customer Success only involved with a subset of customers.	Ad hoc or developing CS tools and operations. CS focus on retention and adoption vs. growth and expansion. Strategic account planning and milestones tracking.

(*continued*)

Table 2-2. (*continued*)

Stage	Relationship	Revenue	Risk	People	Operations
Emerging (Late-stage startup)	Customer segmentation by tiers. White glove dedicated CS engagement only for top-tier customers. Optimizing CX based on customer tier and strategy (hybrid, tech touch, etc.)	All of above + Potential for monetizing services, education and enablement	Customer loss to more established brands. Scaling without shifting focus from customer business outcomes and CX to ARR/NRR to meet growth demands from investors and board. Leading churn indicators and churn risk modelling. Equal investment in CS vs. more in Sales.	Customer Success team expanded to include sub-function leads for Services, Account Management, Consulting, Education etc.	Formalization of CS processes, playbooks and tools. Customer journey milestones tracking. Onboarding and first time to value tracking. Customer Health metrics dashboards. Hot Issues dashboard. Customer segmentation and revenue dashboards and CS pipeline tracking

Enterprise	All of the above from late startups plus Formalizing customer listening posts and Voice of Customer (VoC) initiatives. Customer Advisory Boards Events like user conferences, dedicated customer onsite events. Co-marketing, co-branding initiatives	All of the above plus Optional retention and/or upsell/cross sell quota. Global expansion with regional focus with big customers Sophisticated revenue forecasting/ prediction tools	All of the above plus Annual churn forecasting per customer tier/ segment	All of the above plus Customer Success evolution heatmaps (across different geos of your company) CS tooling and processes standardization across all geos. Advanced enablement via training portals and certifications for customers and partners

CHAPTER 2   CS BUSINESS AND OPERATIONAL MODELS

Now that you have mapped the right business, company, and Customer Success maturity models to your current company, let us briefly introduce an emerging business model that is the next leap forward for Customer Success as part of its 3.0 evolution.

The Customer-Centric Business Model

Customer Success 3.0 is a fundamental shift from product-centric to customer-centric and customer-led growth models with emphasis on standardization and scale.

Customer centricity means putting the customer at the center of your business model. You start by identifying the needs of an individual customer and build a product/delivery model to meet the needs of that customer everywhere, including product, marketing, and so on. This is an evolving business model that is not widely adopted at this time.

Michael Merit, Chief Customer Officer at Planet Labs, an American public Earth imaging company that deploys miniature space satellites to collect and provide up-to-date information to its customers on areas like climate monitoring, crop yield prediction, urban planning, and disaster response, talks about the customer-centric business model in the following way:

> *Customer Centricity is at the core of everything we do here at Planet Labs. Our customer use cases and data requirements directly drive our business and operational models. Adopting this approach has enabled us to evolve to a customer-led high growth model by keeping our top customer profiles and their needs front and center when determining strategies and priorities of functions like Product, Engineering Marketing, CS and Support. We have transformed into a customer led company and the results are very clear. Dramatically higher NPS, Net Retention and Gross Retention resulting in significant margin improvements.*

We will look at the customer-centric and customer-led growth models in more detail in Chapter 10. Let us now return to the question with which we kicked off this chapter, that is, where should your Customer Success organization roll up to?

The Million-Dollar Question

When Customer Success was introduced, depending on the company and the scope of its functionality, it could roll up to Marketing or Sales or Support, or to the CEO or COO. Customer Success should, in an ideal state, be responsible for a customer's entire post-sales/post-win experience and retention. This includes account management, services, support, consulting, and enablement, among others. However, we see many variations in the post-sales customer engagement model where Customer Success sometimes gets slotted exclusively as a post-sales account management or an orchestration function.

There's wide agreement that Customer Success should be a stand-alone function rolling up directly to the CEO or CRO as opposed to another function like Sales or Marketing. Hence the evolution of the role of Chief Customer Officer. The logic being that the Customer Success focus areas of maximizing NRR, desired outcomes, value realization, and experience is done best if not burdened by the overarching goals of other functions.

For example, if CS was rolling up to Sales or Marketing then the primary goals of Sales (grow new revenue) or Marketing (grow new leads), could influence the priorities of Customer Success, which should be focusing on maximizing investment from, and investment of, existing customers. We will explore the structure of an evolving CS Org. and the role of the CCO in Chapters 8 and 10.

In this chapter, we've reviewed organizational structures and customer engagement models based on company maturity. Were you able to map these models to your current organizational structure? Do you see any gaps? Augment the information you already have with the information in this chapter to get a holistic perspective of how you might structure your Customer Success organization and its operations based on business type, company maturity, and customer profiles.

In the next chapter, we will start laying the building blocks for your CS operational model and CS CoE. We will review key processes and workflows in a Customer Success organization, discuss ways to optimize and templatize CS playbooks and delve into the different CS responsibility models.

CHAPTER 3

Key Customer Success Workflows and Processes

Once you've established a CS Org., you need to work out how the Org. interacts with other parts of the company. In other words, who takes on which responsibilities?

In our fictional company SoftCorp, the Sales team previously managed the end-to-end customer experience, from identifying prospects to closing deals and managing customer retention and expansion. When the Customer Succccess(CS) Org. was introduced, key questions had to be answered and decisions made about the scope and roles and responsibilities of this new organization.

Those questions included: At what stage would CS take over the management of customer accounts from Sales? What are the key workflows that CS would define and drive, and how? To answer them, Janice, the CCO, conducted a series of brainstorming sessions with her Sales counterpart, CS leaders, and other key stakeholders. Together, they identified the use cases, hand-off points and workflows to kickstart the CS Practice. Those workflows and processes also became the foundation for the standardization and scaling initiatives driven by the CS CoE operationally.

CHAPTER 3   KEY CUSTOMER SUCCESS WORKFLOWS AND PROCESSES

In this chapter, we will cover some of the key processes and workflows in a CS Org. We will discuss playbooks for critical workflows like customer journey mapping, customer onboarding, and strategic account management. We will also look at how to templatize and optimize these workflows for efficiency and scale, as well as the roles and responsibilities of different team members. Having a good understanding of these concepts is required to build out the foundational components of your CS Org and your CS CoE function.

Building standardized, repeatable, and scalable workflows is key to operationalizing a CS practice, irrespective of the size of the company and current product and company maturity. Setting up the CS practice foundations the right way with an eye for standardization, optimization, and scale will remove the need for costly reorgs and reworks as a company grows and matures.

At the end of this chapter, you will be able to determine the Customer Success workflows that are the best fit for your business models (identified in Chapter 2) based on your company stage and other factors. You will also be able to review workflow templates and optimization opportunities and review CS roles and responsibilities breakdown options to assess a potential fit for your current situation.

Common Decision Points

Before you start building your CS workflows, it is important to understand the scope and responsibilities of your Customer Success Org. and resolve any points of confusion. When you're designing CS workflows, an important question, and in some cases a point of confusion, is when is a customer account designed as "post-sales/post-win" and why? Shouldn't there be a constant focus on growing the customer till they reach their CLV (customer lifetime value)? Or is a customer designated as "post-sales" when we "max out" their CLV and they are in retention mode only?

CHAPTER 3   KEY CUSTOMER SUCCESS WORKFLOWS AND PROCESSES

While there are a myriad of opinions on this, typically a customer is designed as "post-sales" or "post-win" once they have signed a contract with your company to purchase your products and/or services, ideally with opportunities to renew. The contract could be long- or short-term and the customer might be nowhere close to their lifetime value (CLV). But the differentiating factor between a prospect and a customer is that the customer has made an investment in your company. And once they make that investment, they are expecting a return on investment (ROI), which will, in most cases, have a direct influence on whether they will expand and/or renew their investment or not.

That is where Customer Success comes into play to make sure that the customer achieves, and ideally exceeds, their expected ROI and to make sure that you maximize the customer experience and loyalty to solidify future renewals, expansions, and overall partnership.

Another common question is: Does having CS involved mean that the Sales rep does not have to be involved anymore to grow the account? The answer to that question is "It depends." We will cover the three common models of operation in the "CSM Responsibilities Models" section later in the chapter.

Finally, as part of your customer-journey mapping exercise, you have to determine the right stage of a customer journey when CS should start getting involved. This is a very common decision point and, from the perspective of seasoned CS practitioners, the answer is "as soon as possible once the prospect shows clear indications of becoming a customer." This is especially true when complex products and solutions-scoping are involved.

Getting the Customer Success team involved early enough so they can vet customer requirements, success criteria, and solutions helps you get ahead of any deployment, on-boarding or delivery issues due to the potential risk of overpromising and under-delivering.

CHAPTER 3   KEY CUSTOMER SUCCESS WORKFLOWS AND PROCESSES

Having Customer Success involved early is especially helpful if you are in a relatively new field like Internet of Things (IoT), where you might be working with companies that do not fully understand the value proposition of your offering. We know of an IoT PaaS company in which Customer Success signs off on the final Sales proposal to the customer before it is presented. The CS Org. offers consulting services for different phases of the customer journey, some of which are tailored for the pre-sales phase. It helps customers flush out their business solutions or goes through a discovery process to do a requirements/tech feasibility study and build out a proposal for the decision-maker.

These types of consulting services have minimum barriers of entry in terms of both cost and obligation to purchase your products. But they could go a long way in converting prospects into customers faster and also setting up those customers for success by potentially reducing the first time to value. A deep understanding of the customer's setup and the problems they are trying to solve can be obtained from the information that was gathered as part of the consulting engagement in the pre-sales phase.

Tip   Sketching out your ideal and most common customer journeys will provide you with a good snapshot of the process and technology gaps that Customer Success could help fill, in pre- and post-sales stages in both business and technical consulting areas.

Now that we have reviewed some of the important questions and decision points to flush out the scope and R&R of your CS practice, let's look at some of the key processes and workflows you will have to define based on your business model.

CHAPTER 3 KEY CUSTOMER SUCCESS WORKFLOWS AND PROCESSES

Key Processes

Customer Journey Mapping

The post-sales/post-win customer journey is the cornerstone of the Customer Success function. So getting your customer journey right, and making sure you understand all its nuances to offer an exceptional customer experience, is key for both Customer Success leaders and team members.

In this section, we will review a few examples of post-sales customer journey maps, the different phases, and common activities. The way you build your own journey maps could differ based on your organizational and product complexity.

Customer Journey Stages

Table 3-1 shows the typical customer journey phases with some key tasks identified.

CHAPTER 3 KEY CUSTOMER SUCCESS WORKFLOWS AND PROCESSES

Table 3-1. Customer Journey Stages

Pre-sales (optional)	Sales CS handoff/ alignment	Customer onboarding	Ongoing strategies and engagement	Retention and Expansion
Sales team runs customer proposal (including customer use cases and motivations to purchase) by Customer Success team for sign off	Sales-CS knowledge transfer meeting scheduled by Sales when customer is ready for onboarding) Sales fills out customer intake info Sales introduces Customer Success Manager (CSM) to customer CSM takes over onboarding and post-sales account and relationship management OR CSM completes onboarding and hands over account to Sales after onboarding (if CS is not managing the accounts long-term)	Pre-onboarding call with primary customer stakeholder to get aligned on onboarding call planning and customer success criteria (optional call but highly recommended) Send welcome kit to all customer stakeholders (automated or manual) Schedule onboarding call with all relevant stakeholders Capture customer desired goals, business outcomes and timelines Get Customer sign-off on onboarding R&R and schedule Track onboarding progress and complete	Scheduling of customer checkpoints Strategic account planning (QoQ strategy and goals) Execution and monitoring of customer deployment and enablement strategy as defined in the strategic account plan Periodic strategic business reviews (SBR) Outcomes/value attainment customer updates (status reports) Customer health monitoring, retention and mitigation as needed	Customer health reporting and analytics Annual growth strategy and goals setting (Strategic Account Plans can be used for this) Exploring expansion opportunities beyond current customer teams (Sales) Bi-Yearly NPS and CSAT

44

In an ideal as a service (aaS) scenario, there would be a constant loop back between different phases of a customer journey map as the customer expands more and more. Now that you have a clear understanding of the high-level phases of the customer journey, let's look at some examples of how customer-journey maps are built based on the needs of different companies.

Customer Journey Mapping Examples
Example 1: Basic Customer Journey Map

A real example of a company's customer journey map is shown in Figure 3-1. This company is just starting the Customer Success function and wants to map out the high-level customer engagement touchpoints and workflows to flush out the Sales-CS R&R and define customer experience.

The post-sales customer journey starts with the introduction of CSM after the Sales-CS knowledge transfer is complete. The CSM then drives the customer's onboarding process, followed by ongoing engagement activities like conducting project checkpoints and business reviews.

CHAPTER 3   KEY CUSTOMER SUCCESS WORKFLOWS AND PROCESSES

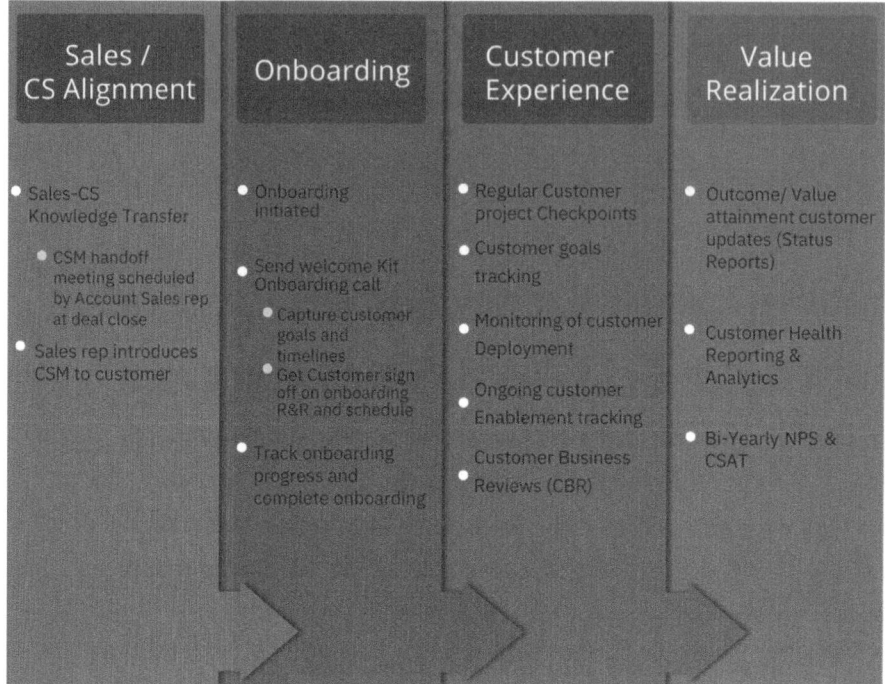

Figure 3-1. Example of a basic customer journey map

All of this aids in maximizing customer outcomes and value realization by leveraging a combination of manual and data-driven engagement approaches. This is an example of journey mapping at its simplest. More complex journey maps, as shown in Figure 3-2, can be built by expanding on this simple but core journey map.

CHAPTER 3 KEY CUSTOMER SUCCESS WORKFLOWS AND PROCESSES

Example 2: Customer Journey Map Broken Down by Functional Responsibilities

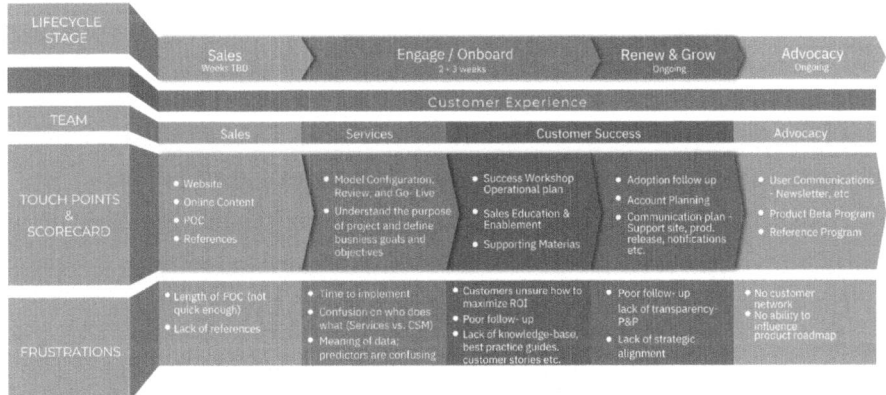

Figure 3-2. Example of an expanded journey map

In this example, as shown in Figure 3-2, the customer journey is mapped in more detail. It not only identifies the top-level customer journey phases (Sales/Engage/Grow etc.) but also flushes out the touchpoints with different internal teams and identifies points of frustration. For example, the Services team assists with onboarding for two to three weeks by defining business goals and doing the configurations. This is important to make sure that onboarding does not take too long. The customer needs to be clear about the scope of involvement of the Services team to avoid any confusion later.

Example 3: Customer Product Journey Mapping for Complex Deployments

Figure 3-3 shows a real-life example of a customer journey map that was built by an Internet of Things (IoT) Platform as a Service (PaaS) company to help its customers launch IoT products on the company's platform. Since IoT is a new field, many customers might be unfamiliar with it.

They might need education, guidance, and close involvement from CS teams to set them up for success throughout their development and launch life cycle. Hence this journey map mirrors the customer's own product development phases like design decision points, development, and launch.

In this example (Figure 3-3), the customer journey is represented as a set of horizontal paths (top-down and left to right). The leftmost chevrons call out the key goals of that row of tasks. For example, the first row (The Essentials) is focused on Customer Education, that is, what kind of information a customer needs to learn about the new industry.

The subsequent rows focus on what processes (Strategy Workshops) and decision points (Decision Models) customers need to invoke or steps they should consider for bringing their first IoT products to market. The final row (Launch Prep and Production) covers the Production process and the life cycle once the first products are in the market.

Building out a customer journey like the following, that is focused on a customer's evolution, from early education and training to achieving desired goals of go-to-market products and solutions, and the steps needed to get there, provides a clear view of how your products fit into this journey. It shows where the gaps might be and how those gaps can be potentially plugged by Customer Success and Consulting services.

CHAPTER 3 KEY CUSTOMER SUCCESS WORKFLOWS AND PROCESSES

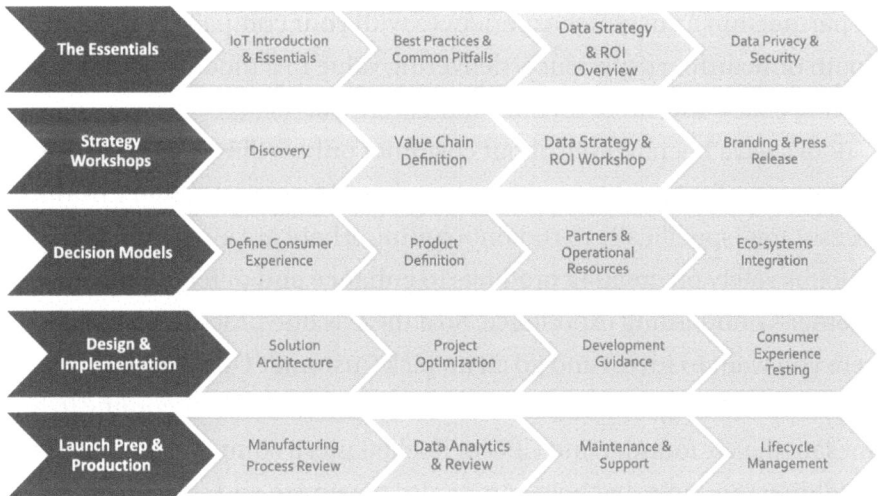

Figure 3-3. Example of an IoT PaaS company's journey map

Now that we've looked at different examples of customer journey maps, let us dig a little deeper into the customer onboarding phase of the customer experience journey map.

Customer Onboarding

Customer onboarding is unarguably one of the most important processes in a customer's journey. Onboarding is when the customer gets their first taste of what a long-term relationship with your company might look like. It is also the phase when customers form their first and lasting impressions about your company. This is the phase where metrics like Customer Perceived Value (CPV) and initial churn risks start taking shape. These first impressions that the customers form can be powerful and long lasting.

Onboarding is an important part of CS, especially considering the importance of reducing time for the customer's first time to first value and its correlation with their growth and expansion. Onboarding is the first partnership a customer experiences with your company, and hence a smooth onboarding experience, delivering value in a timely manner, and reducing chaos and stress on both sides is critical.

Books have been written about customer onboarding methodologies and Customer Success leadership roles are being created within Customer Success Orgs. specifically to run onboarding. There are even companies that focus solely on creating products to enhance and differentiate a customer's onboarding experience. So if there is one process/playbook where you want to invest and go all in, pick Customer Onboarding.

Bad onboarding is the top reason for customer churn, according to Sri Ganesan, the co-founder and CEO of Rocketlane, a company that focuses on building products that help companies maximize and scale their customer onboarding experience.

"Bad implementations have left many SaaS industry verticals, like HR Tech, CRM, etc., scarred forever. The onus is on businesses to set a new standard for their customer onboarding experience. They need to work toward delivering on the original promise of SaaS, 'Easy to set up, and faster time-to-value'. Consistent and reliable onboarding is truly a differentiator, and companies these days are even doing PR about their new onboarding methodologies!" he says.

Sri provides a structured approach to building and scaling your customer onboarding process that is covered in Chapter 4.

A key activity of the onboarding process is to build out the customer's Strategic Account Plan or Success plan. It is a critical step in operationalizing your CS strategy. Account Plans should be built as part of the onboarding process, but they are live documents that are relevant throughout the customer's life cycle. They should be continually updated to capture the customer's requirements and your own strategy to address those requirements to maximize your business goals and those of your customers.

Strategic Account Planning

A Strategic Account Plan provides a snapshot of the customer's organizational setup, primary stakeholders, key use cases, a customer's desired outcomes and success motivators, and a high-level action plan for the next few quarters, including tasks, owners, and important milestones.

In the early days of Customer Success, many Customer Success Orgs. were run with a focus on managing customers' day-to-day operations without proper longer-term strategic planning. The strategic planning was primarily owned by the Sales team and developed at a very high level with a goal of increasing sales. Strategic Account Planning is now a joint initiative between Sales and CS in many companies. There is greater collaboration between the two teams with increased focus on maximizing customers' current goals, instead of focusing solely on growth activities. We have seen that Strategic Account Plans, when properly designed and deployed via CS tools, can help empower your CS predictive analytics and financial models with qualitative data that is tied directly to your customer's success, offering more realistic and accurate assessments of a customer's overall health and expansion probability.

Table 3-2 shows a template for a combined Customer Strategic Account and Success Plan. It consists of customer background information, important use cases, success criteria, risk, opportunities, etc. You can adopt the template to your specific organizational needs.

Table 3-2. Sample Template for a Strategic Account Plan

How is <customer> using your products and services?	*List applications, use cases – if too many to list here, call out the most important ones and create a table and list the rest below.*
Customer groups interfacing	*List all customer teams that work with your company and any details of their areas of focus.* **Note:** *If this list is too big and it makes sense to break strategy by group, please create group-specific overview tables to capture individual success criteria, action plan, and milestones (could be applicable for big customers with multiple groups working with you in parallel).*
How is <customer> using competitors (if info available)?	
Customer leadership/decision-makers	*List info of primary customer leadership team, designation, contact info. Full list should be available in your CRM. Please list only the primary ones here.*
Other stakeholders	*Other stakeholders that your account team interacts with frequently and their roles.*
High-level business goals for <customer>	*These are the customer's own business goals for the current year and near future. Could be independent of their association with your company.*
High-level technology goals for <customer> in 2021	*These are the customer's own technology goals for the current year and near future. Could be independent of their association with your company.*

(*continued*)

Table 3-2. (*continued*)

Customer's success criteria	• *Any time or milestone or outcome-based criteria by which customers will be measuring their success.* • *Success criteria should be associated with the preceding identified goals wherever possible.*

Risks (to your company)
Remove any sub-sections that might not apply and add any that are missing.
	• **Competitive**
	  • *Competitor sprawl?*
	  • *Specific competitor info, if any*
	• **Technology**
	  • *Build vs. Buy Strategy?*
	  • *TCO concerns?*
	  • *Technology compatibility concerns?*
	• **Product**
	  • *Quality issues*
	  • *Product Gaps if any?*
	• **Business**
	  • *Risks based on customer's business goals*
	• **Account management**
	  • *Risks with current account management setup*

Opportunities and desired outcomes for your company	*<these are opportunities and desired outcomes for your company>* *Please try to be as specific as possible so these can be tied to actions, timelines, and deliverables in the action plan.*
Action plan for Q1 and Q2 2021	*You can elaborate high-level plan here and use Table 3-2-1 to call out specific actions and ownerships.*

(*continued*)

Table 3-2. (*continued*)

Success metrics to measure (for internal team)	*Could include:* • *CSAT increase* • *Awareness reach out increase (by no. of teams)*
Account team *For Account team responsibilities, please see Appendix.*	• Sales rep • CSM: • SE: • SA: • Support tier: Gold/Silver/Platinum, etc.

Table 3-2-1. *Example of High Priority Tasks for Current Quarter (Updated Every Quarter with Latest Info)*

High priority tasks for Q1 2021	Owner	Status	Date completed/ETA
Finalize post-sales engagement plan	CS	Done	
Start monthly customer reports	CS	Done	

Conduct awareness sessions
• Competitive review
• Product differentiation
   • Mobile
   • Analytics
	Sales	TBD	

Finalize partner strategy	Sales	TBD	
Build relationships in groups beyond <ABC>	Sales	TBD	

Table 3-2-2. *High Priority Features <Optional>*

High Priority Features	Impact	Owner	Status	ETA for Delivery

Table 3-2-3. *High-Level Applications/Use Cases*

App/use case name	Customer owner	Description	No. of servers

> **Tip** Please note, there are many templates for creating strategic account plans. So feel free to explore and pick one that best suits your business needs. At a minimum, a strategic account plan should provide a snapshot of the customer profile, main points of contact, business motivations to work with your company, success criteria, and major upcoming milestones.

Customer Process Playbooks

Once you identify your customer's post-sales/post-win journey, you can flush out each phase of the journey to create detailed playbooks. The purpose of the playbooks is to create standard, repeatable processes with relevant repurposable artifacts like slide decks and checklists plugged in. Creating detailed playbooks is an important step to optimize, scale, and automate your customer engagement processes and workflows.

When we built CS Orgs, one of our top goals was to offer our customers a reliable, consistent experience in a cost-effective manner. Hence we made sure that we invested early in building out our customer journey maps and playbooks. Every Customer Success Manager (CSM) in the company was trained on using these playbooks as part of the new hire training. They were expected to follow the playbooks steps faithfully, but with room to improvise as needed. As a result, we found it very easy to scale and shuffle CSMs from accounts if needed, with minimal disruption to the customer experience. That's because all the CSMs engaged with customers in a standard way, thanks to the playbooks.

CHAPTER 3 KEY CUSTOMER SUCCESS WORKFLOWS AND PROCESSES

Not all your workflows and processes might need detailed playbooks and artifacts, though most should have some minimal repeatable tasks/processes/activities that can be converted into a playbook and deployed in CS tools. Some of the common CS playbooks used in many companies are shown in Table 3-3.

Table 3-3. Common CS Playbooks

Playbook name	Related artifacts	Owner	Applicable customer journey stage(s)	Deployed in tools
Customer onboarding	Support portal Enablement portal Onboarding deck	CSM	Onboarding	Onboarding and/or CS tool
Renewal onboarding/ refresher	Onboarding refresher deck or webinar		Engagement and Expansion	
Strategic business review (SBR)	SBR process and best practices doc SBR template deck Customer health dashboard Customer health scores	CSM	Engagement and expansion	CRM tool CS tool

(*continued*)

Table 3-3. (*continued*)

Playbook name	Related artifacts	Owner	Applicable customer journey stage(s)	Deployed in tools
Customer project management	Project requirements and execution templates Project planning and scheduling document	Project manager, deliver manager	Onboarding New projects as part of engagement and expansion	Project and time-tracking tool
Consulting workshops (create a row for every workshop with relevant artifacts)	Workshop templates calling out deliverables, R&R, timelines	CSM or business consultant (could be same person)	Pre-sales Onboarding Engagement and Expansion	Project tracking tool
Strategic Account Planning	Strategic Account Plan template	Sales rep and/or CSM	Engagement and Expansion	CS tool that support strategic account planning
Escalation management	Incident management checklist, engineering escalation process doc, etc.	Support and CSM	Any stage	CS tool, Support/Eng tools like JIRA

Playbooks are living, breathing documents. They evolve as your company's products, customers, and maturity evolve. Our preferred style of creating playbooks is shown in the escalations management playbook example in Table 3-4.

Table 3-4. Escalation Management Playbook

Process name	Description	Owner(s)	Assets
Incidence management	A master flow of how Support and Field teams handle incoming incident	Support	Incident Management Flow.pdf
Outage support	Platform issue escalation – Customer Support to DevOps	Support	TS – Procedure – platform issue escalation – Customer Success to development operations
Engineering escalation (Investigation)	A flow of filing a support ticket – Escalation to engineering for further investigation	Field team (tech services engineer)	Engineering Escalation (Investigation) Process Flow.pdf
CSM escalation process	A flow of how a CSM can escalate customer issues to Support/PSE teams	CSM	CSM Escalation Process Flow.pdf

Now that we have identified some of the key workflows and playbooks that might map to your business models, let's look at optimization and scaling techniques that will help you get the most out of your workflows and playbooks.

CHAPTER 3 KEY CUSTOMER SUCCESS WORKFLOWS AND PROCESSES

Optimizing Playbooks for Efficiency and Scale

In this section, we will cover process optimization techniques to help enhance and scale your CS practice. In this context, optimization means tweaking or enhancing existing workflows to fit your customer tiers, company maturity, or business type. If done properly, it helps streamline and scale your existing playbooks to help standardize and scale your Customer Success footprint to all your customers.

Here is an example of how a company did this successfully in real life. After establishing the foundational end-to-end CS practice focused on the top 25% of its customers, this company decided to expand its CS footprint to all customers in the onboarding phase. The company leveraged its existing onboarding playbooks to create a digital touch onboarding playbook. It was driven by an automated, self-serve engagement model and used artifacts like automated welcome emails, onboarding videos, and minimal manual touchpoints.

You can use the following tables as a reference when flushing out your CS workflows and playbooks to plug in the right optimization techniques. Tables 3-5, 3-6, and 3-7 cover optimization techniques per customer tier, company maturity, and business type.

Table 3-5. Optimizations per Customer Tier

Process	Strategic customers	Enterprise customers	All other customers
New Customer Onboarding	• High touch by dedicated CSM • Regular check ins with main point of contact (min. once a month) • Use Standard Account/Success Plan template • Start building your account plan during onboarding itself and get customer sign-off • Actively track milestones identified in plan in regular check-ins with the customer • Leverage all available automations, dashboards and tools to augment CX • Provide customer with a C360 view/portal of their engagement • Send monthly status reports capturing important customer milestones as well as highlights from your side like recent product updates, competitive info, etc. (Consider building a tool to automatically pull this info for your customers)	• Hybrid onboarding model with automated onboarding (onboarding survey, welcome kit, self-serve portals, etc.) and one customer touchpoint with a CSM to sign-off success plan • CS experience offered via a common pool of CSMs, who use tools to monitor and track customer's health and progress and reach out to the customer as needed. • Dedicated CSM could be assigned to some accounts, but touchpoints not as frequent as strategic customers	• Tech touch auto onboarding with standard steps and tool-driven onboarding (auto emails, reminders of key tasks, related artifacts), etc.

Onboarding refreshers for new team members of existing customers	• High touch and done case by case as new teams get onboarded	• Offer common onboarding refresher webinars • Share recorded sessions of core onboarding processes	• Offer onboarding refresher webinars • Share recorded sessions of core onboarding processes like Support portal/ training portal set ups.
Monthly customer status updates and syncs	• In-person syncs by dedicated CSM • Auto generation and propagation of monthly performance updates	• Auto generation and propagation of monthly performance updates	• Auto generation and propagation of monthly performance updates

(*continued*)

Table 3-5. (*continued*)

Process	Strategic customers	Enterprise customers	All other customers
Strategic business reviews	• Onsite strategic business reviews with Customer executive team on a regular cadence	• Quarterly touchpoints with key decision-maker (may not be executive meeting and could be offsite) • Auto generation and propagation of quarterly performance updates	• Auto generation and propagation of quarterly performance updates • Customer touchpoints based on health triggers, industry events, and ahead of renewal (triggers should be automated)
Customer engagement and journey tracking	• Use CS tool to track customer account information and health triggers • CS Dashboard specifically for each customer	• Use CS tool to track customer account information and health triggers • Dashboard level tracking for customer group, regions etc	• Use CS tool to track customer account information and health triggers • Dashboard level tracking for customer groups, regions, etc.

Table 3-6. *Optimizations per Company Maturity*

Workflow	Early-stage startup with < 50 customers	Late-stage startup or mid-size company	Big enterprises
First-time customer onboarding	High touch manual onboarding for all customers	Hybrid approach for customer onboarding with a mix of tech touch/self-serve and manual	Structured customer tier-based onboarding model Pooled CS resources for mid-tier customers and tech-touch for all other customers
Renewal	High touch renewal experience	Renewal refresher sessions and onboardings for new teams as needed	Renewal refresher sessions and onboardings for new teams as needed

(*continued*)

Table 3-6. (*continued*)

Workflow	Early-stage startup with < 50 customers	Late-stage startup or mid-size company	Big enterprises
Customer projects/ deployments (execution)	All hands on deck led by CS leader to make customer successful	Structured approach with services involvement (either paid or unpaid)	Ideally, a paid services involvement with clearly defined operational model
Ongoing customer engagement Regular manual check-ins Status reports Strategic business reviews	Weekly or monthly Custom and semi-manually generated and shared individually for top customers Onsite for top customers	Monthly or quarterly Semi-auto generated and shared manually for top customers and at scale by tool for others Onsite for top customers	Tiered approach — High touch with some automations and tech touch for top customers — Mid touch for enterprise customers — Tech touch for all other customers

Table 3-7. Optimizations per Business Type

Workflow	Plug n Play SaaS	PaaS/IaaS/XaaS
First-time customer onboarding	Automated and self-serve	Semi-automated or automated based on customer tier
Renewal/refresh	Automated monthly or whatever cadence is specified during sign up	Negotiated
Customer projects/ deployments (execution)	Automated and self-serve via portal with paid services as needed	Negotiated if professional services are needed
Ongoing customer engagement Regular manual check-ins Status reports Strategic business reviews	Only as needed Only if needed – provide way to self-download reports As needed for big customers only	CSM decides and drives cadence Could be semi-manual or automated based on customer size As needed for big customers

The Importance of Templatizing Workflows

Standardization and templatization of your workflows and playbooks as much as possible is key for scaling your CS engagement and practice. The first step is to understand how you can incorporate and customize these standard workflows into your own customer journey map. Then you have to determine which of these templates can be incorporated or adapted to your automated workflows for self-serve and auto-tracking.

For example, if your customer has a complex onboarding process with multiple teams and business units being onboarded, you can use a standard template like the one shown in Figure 3-4.

<Customer Name> Onboarding Plan

Account Setup Information						
Customer Teams/Segements	*BU/region*	*Products Purchased*	*Customer Contact/Email*	*Billing Contact/Email*	*Go-Live Budget*	*Go-Live Date*
Identify customer teams, regions etc to onboard if they have to be onboarded individually in seperate rows					$705,000	

Sales Account Manager	*CS Manager*	*Services Manager*	*SME/Advisor*

Pilot Phases and Goals (optional if customer is piloting product on short term trial/contract)			
Phase/Timeline	*Goal(s)*	*Actions*	*Next Steps*
Phase 1/<Enter timeline>			
Phase 2/<Enter timeline>			

Onboarding Steps						
Phase/Step	*Start Date - End Date*	*<Company> Tasks*	*Customer Tasks*	*Milestones*	*Value (Proof)*	*Completion Date*
Phase1/Step 1					<What is being measured> <how is value derived for customer> <use case>	
Phase 1 / Step 2						
Phase 2 / Step 1						

Figure 3-4. *Sample customer onboarding template for complex deployment*

After reviewing CS workflows and playbooks, let's now look at some operational models for Customer Success from the perspective of a CSM's scope of responsibilities.

CSM Responsibility Models

There are different execution models that you can implement based on the roles and responsibilities of different customer-facing teams and which role is the main point of contact for customers. As a best practice, it is good to have a single, primary post-sales point of contact to minimize confusion and ensure optimal customer experience. In this section, we cover some of the common models we see in different companies.

CHAPTER 3   KEY CUSTOMER SUCCESS WORKFLOWS AND PROCESSES

Model 1: Customer Success and Sales Are Joint Account Owners

In this model, the Customer Success Manager (CSM) is handed off the customer account for management by the sales team once the customer is ready to be onboarded. The CSM and sales rep share account ownership. The CSM is responsible for customer onboarding, adoption, experience, and retention and the sales rep is responsible for growth and expansion. The CSM will not carry a sales quota and will be measured on metrics like customer health, adoption, retention, referencability, success stories and CSAT/NPS.

The CSM, as the main point of contact for the customer, can create Customer Success Qualified Leads (CSQLs) to pass on to the Sales team whenever they identify expansion opportunities during the course of their interaction with the customer. In this model, the CSMs are empowered to become business consultants and trusted advisors to their customers.

This is one of the most common CS models today. It clearly helps differentiate the roles and responsibilities (R&R) of the CS team from the Sales team. The CS team is responsible for day-to-day customer engagement, adoption, CX, and retention without any pressure to meet sales quotas for their accounts. The sales team can focus on expansion and growth without worrying about customer outcomes, experience, and value realization. It is a good division of labor, with both teams playing to their strengths.

CHAPTER 3 KEY CUSTOMER SUCCESS WORKFLOWS AND PROCESSES

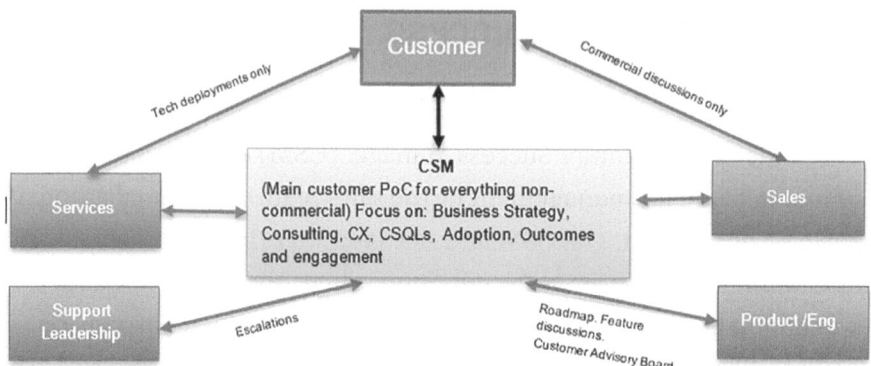

Figure 3-5. *CSM is the main post-sales/win customer point of contact*

As shown in Figure 3-5, the CSM plays the role of the account quarterback and main point of contact for the customer and brings different team members into the conversation as needed. There could be some direct interactions between the customer and the Services and Sales teams for projects or leads discussions, but the scope of these interactions should be tightly controlled to ensure that the customer does not start looking at those teams as their main point of contact.

The primary owners of the different customer engagement workflows for this model are shown in Table 3-8.

Table 3-8. CSM Responsibilities Model 1: R&R Mapping to Workflows

Workflow	Primary owner (can be delegated to other functions as applicable)
Customer onboarding	CS
Customer training planning	CS (delivery could be done by training team)
Customer engagement and health	CS
Customer escalations	CS
Tech projects deliverables	Professional services
Support tickets resolution	Support
Coordination with Product/Engineering	CS
Strategic account planning	CS and sales jointly
Customer churn/retention owner	CS
Customer growth/expansion owner	Sales

CHAPTER 3   KEY CUSTOMER SUCCESS WORKFLOWS AND PROCESSES

Model 2: Customer Success Is Responsible for Process Orchestration and Support

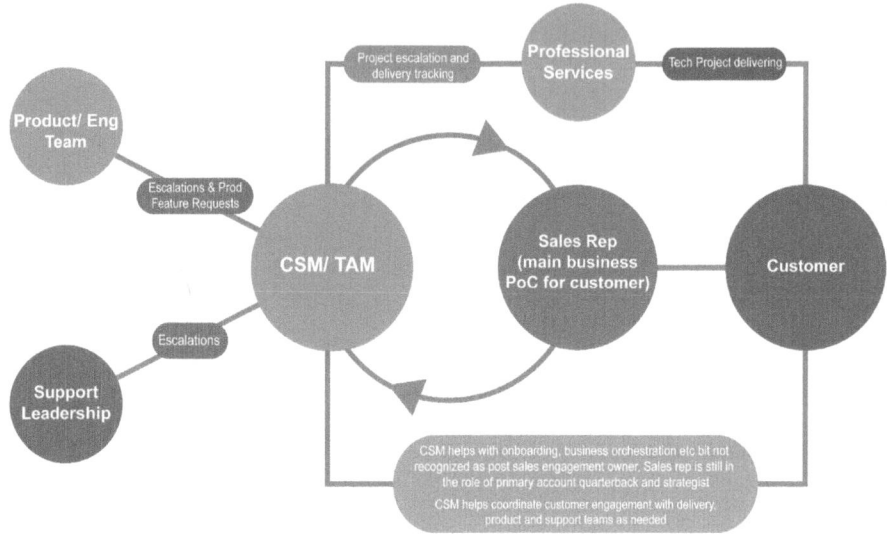

Figure 3-6. *Sales rep is the main post-sales customer point of contact*

In this model, as shown in Figure 3-6, the CSM is involved primarily in support and orchestration mode like a Technical Account Managers (TAM). CSMs help orchestrate escalations and deployments and access to internal teams like Support and Product as needed. They are not involved in post-sales strategic account management and not held accountable for account churn/success or overall customer health.

This model used to be common in the early days of CS when the CS team used to roll up to Support and customer interactions used to be transactional in nature. It is the least preferred model for CS since it does not play to the strengths of Customer Success. The CS team cannot effectively build a strategic trusted advisor relationship and take ownership of activities like adoption and outcomes management proactively.

Table 3-9. CSM Responsibilities Model 2: R&R Mapping to Workflows

Workflow	Primary driver (can be delegated to other functions as applicable)
Customer Onboarding	CS
Customer training planning	CS (delivery could be done by training team)
Customer engagement and health monitoring	CS
Customer escalations	CS
Tech projects deliverables	Professional services
Support tickets resolution	Support
Coordination with Product/Engineering	CS
Strategic account planning	Sales
Customer churn/retention owner	Sales
Customer growth/expansion owner	Sales

Model 3: Customer Success Is Sole Post-sales Account Owner

In this model, as shown in Figure 3-7, along with being the account quarterback and primary point of contact as described in Model 1, the CSM is also responsible for the growth and expansion of the customer account and would carry a growth quota. In this model, the sales team will not be involved with managing or growing the customer beyond the acquisition.

CHAPTER 3 KEY CUSTOMER SUCCESS WORKFLOWS AND PROCESSES

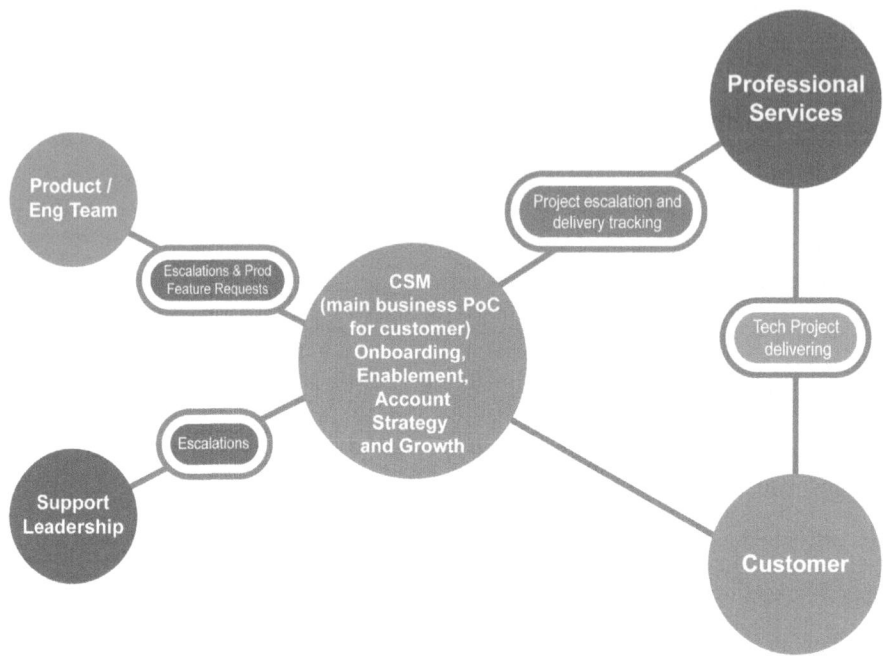

Figure 3-7. *CSM is the sole post-sales customer account owner*

This is an upcoming model in many companies, especially some of the enterprise and strategic companies where CS is being given expansion responsibilities to convert them from a cost center to a profit center. There are pros and cons to this model. On the one hand, the CSM and CS team will have more clout in the company since they are actively generating revenue instead of being a cost center.

However, this model puts CS in a Sales role and there is always the danger of the CS team moving away from its core focus of maximizing customer outcomes and experience in the interest of increasing sales to meet its quotas. Table 3-10 shows the R&R between different cross-functional teams for this play.

Table 3-10. CSM Responsibilities Model 3: R&R Mapping to Workflows

Workflow	Primary driver (can be delegated to other functions as applicable)
Customer onboarding	CS
Customer training planning	CS (delivery could be done by training team)
Customer engagement and health	CS
Customer escalations	CS
Tech projects deliverables	Professional services
Support tickets resolution	Support
Coordination with Prod/Eng	CS
Strategic account planning	CS
Customer churn/retention owner	CS
Customer growth/expansion owner	CS

In this chapter, we've laid the building blocks of your CS practice and operational model. We reviewed key workflows of a Customer Success organization like customer journey mapping, customer onboarding and strategic account management. And we discussed the importance of templatizing and optimizing the CS playbooks. Finally, we looked at the different R&R models for CSMs.

In the next chapter, we will delve deeper into the important workflow of Customer Onboarding. Sri Ganesan, the CEO of Rocketlane, a company that builds cutting-edge customer onboarding technology, outlines his approach to building and scaling customer onboarding methodologies.

CHAPTER 4

Customer Onboarding – A Methodology

Sri Ganesan, CEO Rocketlane

As discussed in Chapter 3, Customer Onboarding is one of the most important workflows in a company's customer journey. In this chapter, Sri Ganesan, the CEO of Rocketlane, a company that builds cutting-edge customer onboarding technology, outlines his approach to building and scaling customer onboarding methodologies.

Let us break down different aspects of onboarding that you may consider as part of your onboarding methodology:

- Kick-off/Introduction
- Planning
- Basic account setup and handover
- Basic configuration
- Implementation and testing (integrations, customization, more config, data migration/setup, custom development, etc.)
- Go-live planning and Go-live

- Training
- In-product guidance/User onboarding
- Adoption planning and monitoring
- Hypercare

Table 4-1 shows how to group Customer Success (CS) and Implementation/Delivery teams roles and responsibilities based on the onboarding approach.

Table 4-1. CS Responsibilities Breakdown Based on Onboarding Approach

Tech touch onboarding	• Automated "Adoption" or "Setup" emails that go out at different times to nudge the customer toward different features they can benefit from or things they need to do to get started • In-product overlays and nudges that guide each user toward completing their setup or feature adoption
Low touch onboarding	• One or two calls where the customer is introduced to their account, key functionality, and any setup help is provided • Typically one setup/kickoff call and one review call post-setup • Email or chat support is encouraged and available during the onboarding phase
High touch onboarding	• Three or more calls with the customer during the onboarding and implementation journey • Active guidance, consulting, or actual work done by the onboarding specialist during the journey • Starts with kickoff, planning the implementation, and then active engagement for implementation, and then active involvement in go-live planning, adoption, training, etc.

So what kind of onboarding should you do? High touch? Tech touch? Should you be holding multiple calls a week to get the customer to value? Or should you enable a self-serve, in-app experience and content for users at the customer side to onboard themselves?

The answer, as always, is that it depends. Your company stage, ideal customer profile (ICP), and LTV (lifetime value of the customer) all determine the best approach for you. If you are an early-stage startup selling to mid-market or enterprise companies, you may want to invest in this high-touch onboarding very early. It raises your credibility, helping you sell more. It allows you to get customers to value faster, and the better upstream journey reduces downstream churn risk. Even if you are selling to SMBs, it is worthwhile having a low/medium touch onboarding in your initial days while you are still understanding how customers engage and adopt your product, what the bottlenecks are, etc.

Table 4-2 outlines the approach I recommend, just considering the stage of the company and customer type:

Table 4-2. *Onboarding Approach Based on Company Stage and Customer Type*

Stage selling to	Seed/series A	Series B/C	Series D+
SMB	Tech touch or Mid touch	Tech touch	Tech touch
Mid-market	High touch	Mid touch	Mid touch
Enterprise	High touch	High touch	High touch

Scaling Your Onboarding

Scaling onboarding does not always mean just tech touch, though tech touch is, of course, an important part of scaling SMB onboarding and the "user onboarding" within the customer account.

CHAPTER 4   CUSTOMER ONBOARDING – A METHODOLOGY

Here are some key steps for scaling your low touch or high touch CSM and Implementation team-driven onboarding.

1. **Design your onboarding methodology**

    The first step to scaling is to have an actual playbook for how you execute. Turn your checklist or steps you send over email/spreadsheets to customers into a project plan of sorts that covers the high-level to low-level activities through the entire journey, from sales to CS handoff, kickoff, planning, implementation, data migration, testing, go-live, training, and first value delivery. Here's a template to give you ideas to get started:

    https://bit.ly/ob-template

2. **Planning and tracking**

    There are specialized tools available for customer onboarding today that help you templatize your playbook into the system and monitor onboarding journey progress with ease.

    Using templated plans and fleshing out each step with the right detail, help content and videos, best practices, etc., ensures that even the newest team member can do those steps as well as your senior team members.

    Templates, like the one shown in Figure 4-1, help create projects with the right start and end date with ease. When you use a system, tracking projects is also easy out of the box. Leaders get quick visibility into what's happening across projects in terms of progress, delays, customer sentiment, BRAG status,

CHAPTER 4   CUSTOMER ONBOARDING – A METHODOLOGY

and more. Onboarding specialists too get a view of their work across projects and are able to easily stay on top of all their work and priorities.

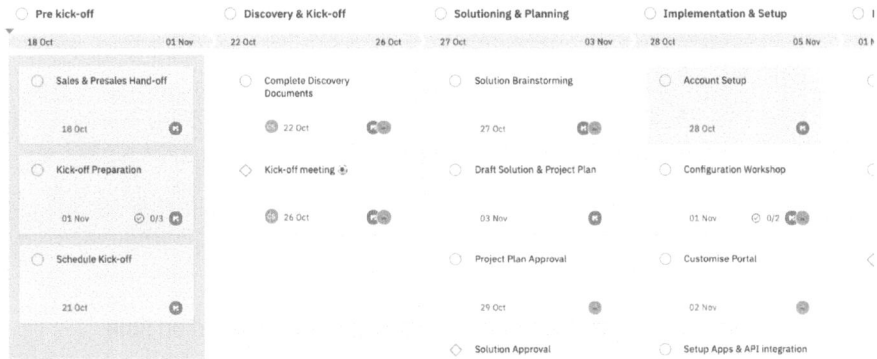

Figure 4-1. Onboarding template

3. **Measure your onboarding**

   While we all measure downstream metrics of health scores and customer engagement levels, we often miss out on measuring the onboarding progress – the most important initial phase where your customers are set up for success. Ensure that completion, time, and feedback for onboarding activities are measured and you have data for what your team did on time vs. what the customer got done.

   You can also see patterns to learn from and iterate on the methodology itself: how to break down activities better, how to remove a bottleneck, where to focus on for more automation, which steps to be more intentional about based on the risk, or the probability of things going wrong. Table 4-3 lists the metrics to measure so that you can actively assess and improve your onboarding.

Table 4-3. *Onboarding Metrics*

Project Metrics	• Time-to-value • 30-60-90 day ROI • % projects completed late • Slippage in end date (number of days) • Actual duration (days) vs. planned duration • Budgeted hours vs. tracked hours • % tasks, % phases, % milestones completed on time • Project delay reasons • Milestone-wise average CSAT and average project CSAT
Activity Metrics	• Tasks, milestones, phases completed late most often • Tasks, milestones, phases completed early most often • Category-wise hours tracked vs. benchmarks/estimates • Top categories on which time was recorded
People Metrics	• % tasks on time vs. late per person • % tasks late on customer • Utilization Rate, Billable Utilization Rate • Distribution of time spent across work categories per person • CSAT per person

4. **Other Key Systems and needs for scaling**

   Learning Management System and Knowledge base

   Video and written content that help during setup, implementation, and training/user onboarding phase by enabling easy access to useful content that aids in scaling the implementation and adoption.

This includes embedding relevant help content as part of the onboarding project plan that references the right content from the account.

In-Product onboarding

In-product guides and content that helps users get contextual tips, inputs, and help through the onboarding journey through bots, user onboarding software, etc.

Automation

- Automate project creation and link with your CRM so closed deals turn into projects without any intervention needed.

- Automate drip emails and nudges to customers through the journey based on their individual context in the journey.

- Reminders, status updates, alerts through the onboarding journey.

Dimensions of Onboarding Maturity

As your team matures, you also want to establish the right practices and behaviors across the team in different dimensions. Here are some questions across dimensions that will help you think about maturity, scaling, and putting together your playbooks:

1. **Communication and CX**

    For a scaling team, you need to establish clear protocols for communication – internal and external.

a. What are the cadences of meetings?

b. Do you have a steering committee with key stakeholders?

c. How are you keeping customers and internal teams posted on updates to the project?

d. What are the cadences of status update emails published to the whole team?

e. What's the protocol around escalations?

f. Are you measuring CSAT through the journey?

g. Do you measure customer effort during onboarding in any manner?

Example Use Case

Pando, a supply chain and logistics start-up, made two changes to its kickoff process that resulted in much greater responsiveness and professionalism from their customers during the onboarding journey:

1. They asked their customers to fix the cadence of Steering Committee meetings with the key customer-side executives right at Kickoff and put it on the core team's calendar.

2. They highlighted their status update mechanisms and escalation protocol for all to be aware of and agree upon.

This helped them move fast and call out issues early, as no one was worried about whether the customer-side points of contacts (PoCs) may be offended by being called out. For any big items that needed resolution of deadlocks or re-scoping, the steering committee was able to provide quick inputs on direction and decisions.

2. **Value Orientation**

   How soon you deliver first-value to the customer determines the customer's affinity and confidence in your solution and company.

   a. How well is your team aligned on the value delivered by your product?

   b. Do all customer-facing teams and internal-facing teams speak the same language with respect to the value delivered?

   c. Are there clear value metrics tracked for every implementation and onboarding project?

   d. Are you measuring time-to-value and the 30-60-90 day ROI?

Example Use Case

At Innovaccer, the team put together a clear formula around value unlocked for the customer based on deployed applications. Customers can see what the value realized is from their implementation and rollout of Innovaccer at any point in time from a customer portal.

3. **Adaptability and Orgs**

   Meet your customers where they are. Your plans need to understand the customer context and remember that companies cannot transform in too many ways at once. If they are at maturity level 1, you can take them to level 2 or 3, not to level 5 in one shot.

    a. Do you have plans and templates for onboarding and implementation?

    b. Are your plans flexible and contextual based on the maturity of the customer?

    c. Do you have a dedicated onboarding/implementation/PS org?

    d. Do you have partners involved in implementations to scale onboarding beyond your internal resources?

Example Use Case

Insent.ai is a chatbot company that supports advanced ABM campaigns to be supported by campaign-aware chatbots. However, it did not focus on this top feature for every customer from the get-go for their onboarding. They divided customers into what they called Gen1 and Gen2.

Gen1 companies were using a chatbot for the first time, and the onboarding plan for them was simply to get the first few bot flows live and the integrations with CRM, Teams, etc. configured.

Gen2 companies were shifting from competitor products, so it was essential to showcase value from the advanced ABM capabilities early.

4. **Manageability and Productivity**

    Measure what you want to influence and change. Metrics to measure your onboarding team and the effectiveness of your processes are important to make progress and recognize areas of improvement.

    a. Do you measure onboarding metrics by team, region, and milestone?

    b. Do you measure task, milestone, and project-related metrics, as well as track time against activities?

    c. Do you have an audit mechanism to review project delivery and engagement quality?

    d. Do you have automation on the project management aspects of follow-ups, status updates, alerts for internal and customer teams?

Do you have an automation strategy around user onboarding, training, data migration, configuration, etc.?

Example Use Case

Leadsquared is a CRM company that actively uses time tracking extensively to understand what activities the team is spending time on, so they can focus on process improvement and automation in the right areas. They also use the effort information to see if the key projects are getting the right amount of attention and if the effort is commensurate with the customer size.

We have laid the foundation stones for your CS CoE by nailing down the CS business and operational models and flushed out the key workflows to operationalize and scale. We are now ready to dive into metrics, dashboarding, automations, and scaling mechanisms to fill out your CS operational model.

CHAPTER 5

Key Metrics and Beyond

What you can't measure, you can't fix.

Metrics are vital to effectively measure the value of a Customer Success organization. But you need to use the right metrics in the right way. To illustrate this, let's consider two different scenarios in which they were not. In the first, a Customer Success executive was responsible for presenting his organization's ROI and accomplishments to the board. His CS CoE was capturing a large quantity of data from extensive listening posts deployed throughout the customer journey. At one point, he had a dashboard with no fewer than 57 different metrics. But there was no clear prioritization or grouping into different themes. This made it very hard for him to demonstrate the value CS provided, even with all that raw data at his disposal.

Another CS leader was in the early days of establishing her CS practice at a mid-size company with a strong sales-driven culture. Indeed, all the existing operations and data-driven metrics were sales-driven. She struggled to access clear metrics due to the lack of defined CS workflows, processes, and tools. And without the right data and KPIs to drive critical decision-making, she struggled to justify the CS Org's existence.

We will address both these scenarios in this chapter by discussing the key metrics to measure the effectiveness of a Customer Success organization. We will also review common CS KPIs and related metrics that are important to capture as part of your customer's lifecycle. At a conceptual level, the central themes of a XaaS (Everything as a service) model are to acquire and then retain and expand the customer footprint on an ongoing basis through a subscription model. The cost of acquiring customers is typically multiples of the cost to retain them (about 8x). While Marketing and Sales spending has become operationalized, it is still difficult for businesses to understand how to fund customer-retention programs effectively to manage for growth. While it is widely agreed that a post-sales/post-win Customer Success function is imperative, the impact of Customer Success in terms of ROI is less clear.

If a business invests $1 on Customer Success, what should it expect in return based on customer revenue or profit? In this chapter, we'll explore the metrics that are important to measure customer retention and growth and how they can be combined to deliver a unified metric that helps measure the ROI of a Customer Success Org.

Before we discuss the key metrics, it's important to be clear about the difference between metrics and key performance indicators (KPIs).

Metrics vs. KPIs

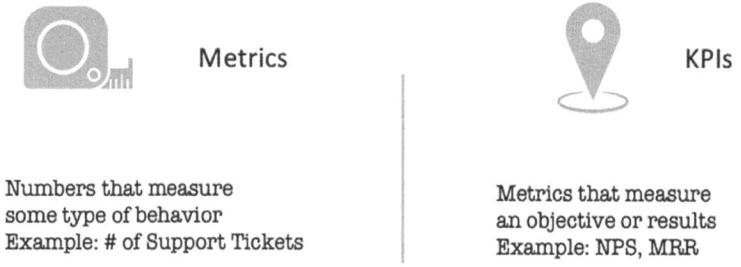

Figure 5-1. *Metrics vs. KPIs*

As shown in Figure 5-1, metrics are quantitative individual data points or numbers that measure a type of behavior. Key Performance Indicators (KPIs), on the other hand, are a set of metrics that, when analyzed or

CHAPTER 5   KEY METRICS AND BEYOND

measured as a set or aggregate, map to a desired outcome or result. So your goal of capturing metrics is to tie them to desired outcomes and the KPIs you are interested in. If that correlation is not made properly, the value of the captured metrics will not be realized to their maximum potential.

When you are looking to identify the right metrics for your KPIs, it is important to understand what type of metrics they are and the broader implications of how those metrics can be used. At an individual level, be clear about your key stakeholders. What are their biases? Do they tend to lead with data or assumptions? Which metrics would be good for them and bad for them and so on. At a group level, understand the goals of specific groups/functions that would be interested in these metrics. Are they lagging or leading? Do you have a say in establishing their goals?

It's also important to understand the difference between Vanity and Actionable metrics. Vanity metrics are metrics that do not offer clear guidance on what actions you need to take based on the results of the metric. NPS is an example of a vanity metric. An NPS score could make your CS Org. look good or not so good, depending on the score. In the absence of correlating it with other relevant data like usage and support tickets, it does not offer clear, actionable insights on how you can use the score to get to a desirable outcome.

Actionable metrics are the statistics that can be used by CSMs to improve business outcomes and demonstrate value to customers. The following are some key definitions that could drive your KPIs and metrics based on your function:

- **Sales:** Profitability, value, productivity

- **Support:** Track interactions, SLA to assist with managing expectations, First contact resolution, Self-help/Case deflection

- **Engineering/Product Management:** Utilization of features, quality of product, Innovation, OLA to backup support, SLA

CHAPTER 5   KEY METRICS AND BEYOND

- **Finance:** Profitability, value, loss, lifetime value (LTV)
- **Customer Success:** Customer satisfaction, renewals, value
- **Other Organizations and Generic:** Metrics for tracking interactions or dependencies, metrics for tracking exceptions

Think back to the opening story of this chapter involving the CS executive whose team was capturing a multitude of metrics. His challenge is to figure out which of those metrics would tie directly to measuring the Customer Success Org Value.

How Do We Measure Customer Success Org. Value?

Figure 5-2. Customer org. value calculation metrics

CHAPTER 5   KEY METRICS AND BEYOND

The best way to justify the value, and hence the budget, for your Customer Success Org. is to quantify the efforts, effects, and impact. And the first step for any quantification or measurement is to a) identify the right metrics and b) find a way to track and capture the relevant data to calculate the preceding metrics. Figure 5-2 shows some of the most important and widely used KPIs in the CS practice. We will explore these in detail in this chapter.

Customer Lifetime Value (CLV/LTV) and Churn Rate

By definition, Customer Lifetime Value is calculated as annual revenue per customer (adjusted for gross margin) related to the churn rate. The greater the customer lifetime length (in months), the greater their value and profitability contribution through their lifetime.

Customer Lifetime Value (CLV/LTV) = {(Average MRR) X (Gross Margin%)}/(Churn Rate)

In this equation, "Churn Rate" is the combined outcome of all customer interactions and touchpoints – that is, onboarding, customer support, product fit, services delivery, relationship management.

Similarly, "Average Revenue per Account" is the combined outcome of customer revenue growth through cross-sells and up-sells. Customer Lifetime Value therefore is a function of both a customer experience metric as well as a post-sale/win expansion metric.

A dollar invested in Customer Success will thereby impact either the churn rate or the average revenue per customer, depending on the functional area the investment is in – retention or expansion.

Tracking these metrics and correlating them to CLV delivers a clear measure of value creation. In order to increase CLV, investments have to be made either in MRR expansion (account management) or MRR protection (customer success, support, services, training). As the ratio of CLV to CAC (Customer Acquisition Cost) improves, a SaaS business trends toward profitability. (Note: In the desirable event that a SaaS company achieves negative churn (i.e., $ expansion > $ churned), the CLV calculation ceases to be representative.)

Customer Churn

Calculating churn can be simple or complicated depending on how accurate you want your churn rate to be. Customer churn assesses the number of paying customers lost from a cohort during a defined period. A simple way to calculate the churn rate for a defined period can be as follows:

Customer Churn Rate for a defined time period = (Total no. of active customers at beginning of time period − No. of churned customers)/Total no. of active customers at the beginning of time period

Churn management is about identifying customers who are likely to churn and proactively taking steps to retain them by tracking the reasons your customers churn and taking appropriate mitigating action.

Customer Health Score

Customer Health Score is a very important data point(s) and metric for not only the Customer Success organization but also for your whole company. There is no fixed formula for calculating the Customer Health Score. Different companies apply different formulae and metrics to calculate this score. It can be both quantitative and qualitative.

If there is a concern shared by Customer Success professionals, it is determining customer health scores in real-time in order to have good leading churn indicators to head off churn before it gets to a tipping point. Having a Customer Health Scoring System that can analyze ongoing changes to the score could be a game changer. You can then highlight the underlying factors causing those changes, and, most importantly, make recommendations for what can be done well ahead of time.

A Customer Success scorecard can either be a score from 0 to 10 or colors like red, green, and yellow to indicate customer health. If equipped with the right data and algorithm, it can even give the reason why your customer is happy or unhappy, their product usage, their experience during recent interactions, and other details about your customers. It can be one of the most valuable tools in your CS arsenal.

Here is a real-life example of how a data and analytics tools company transformed their CS practice by leveraging health score data. The company had continually refined their customer health score tracking by leveraging CS tools and analytics to a point where they now have a data-driven, automated customer health scoring system that is predictable enough to be a valuable leading indicator for churn. Initially, they started using this scoring system to validate and score churn risks for their bottom 30% of customers based on which they bucketed customers as "definitely churn," "likely churn," etc. Based on this ranking, they proactively addressed the controllable risks via war rooms and other mitigating actions to help reduce churn by 40+%. This approach was so successful that they expanded the automated customer health score tracking to all their customers.

Here is how the company's Head of CS described the evolution of their customer health scoring system *"We have found our current health scoring system to be so valuable that we are now expanding it to include multiple prediction models including persona and feature level usage into our health scores. We expect this to help us take our customer health predictability to the next level through this customer centric approach to health scoring."*

For each company, and potentially for each type of customer, your customer scoring system could need varying inputs. And a key question usually is what weightage should you give to the selected metrics that make up the health score?

CHAPTER 5 KEY METRICS AND BEYOND

Along with the current metrics and mapping progress toward the customer's desired business outcomes, it is also important to capture historical scores to capture past trends and patterns of experience and behavior, as shown in Figure 5-3. It shows a sample scoring model to build your customer health scores.

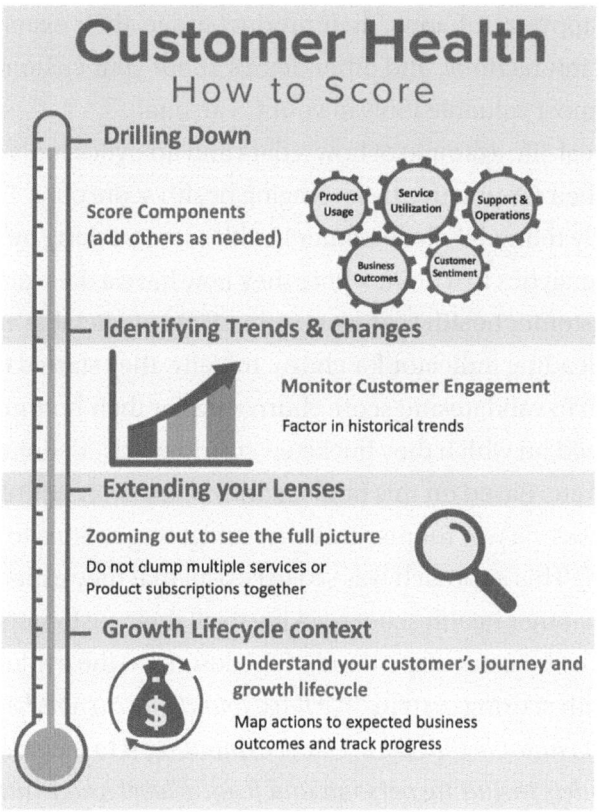

Figure 5-3. Customer health scoring

CHAPTER 5   KEY METRICS AND BEYOND

Some of the best practices to keep in mind to build out your customer health score are

- **Identify which criteria are important for your company to incorporate into the customer health score.** While the actual metrics would depend on your business model and product offerings, some of the common ones are First Time to Value (deployment), Level of Engagement (Engagement), Product Adoption (Adoption), perceived and actual ROI from their investment (ROI), etc.

- **Consider Perceived vs. actual ROI/Value** because there could be a difference between the two based on the customer's opinion or sentiment about your company. One of the responsibilities of the Customer Success team is to understand if there is a difference between the value the customer perceives to be getting from your company and the actual value and if that gap needs to be plugged.

- **Identify Trends and Changes in Behavior.** Not all customers engage the same way. So we cannot use the same baseline to measure customer behavior. Create a customer-specific baseline of their engagement model and track changes to this behavior to reflect in the customer health score and also to create triggers and/or raise flags as needed.

- **Zoom out** and look at the big picture of the customer's journey and engagement. How is their engagement distributed across geographies or functions or products and do their expectations vary? Wherever it makes sense, do not clump multiple product or services subscriptions together since expectations from the individual subscriptions, the stakeholders involved, and expected ROI might be different. In such cases, it makes sense to treat them as separate sub-customers and track their health individually.

- **Growth Life Cycle Context**

    Along the same lines as the preceding, determine if the customer's desired outcomes, ROI expectations are being met and if and growth projections need to be segmented and treated differently for different business units or regions or based on different product/services subscriptions.

Customer Loyalty (Net Promoter Score)

NPS is a customer loyalty metric that asks the question – "How likely are you to recommend Product or Service X to a friend?" The answers are on a scale between 1 and 10, with 1 as least likely, and 10 most likely to recommend the product or service. Many companies use NPS to measure customer satisfaction. You could apply the NPS question for the entire company or conduct NPS surveys for specific functions and areas like Support, Services, and Customer Success specifically.

In some cases, an NPS survey can be combined with a CSAT survey to gather well-rounded and robust customer feedback with actionable data. The appendix has a sample NPS/CSAT survey that you can repurpose to suit your needs. By monitoring these metrics and other important ones, you will be able to gather valuable data to make a strong case to the executive team for growing and scaling your Org.

Product Activity Score

Product Activity Score measures how your products are being used and consumed by your customers. In a nutshell, it tracks usage and adoption. Depending on your company's offerings portfolio, there are different ways of calculating this score. At its simplest, you could map it directly to your product usage and consumption analytics.

For example, let's say that you are a company that provides cloud infrastructure and storage services. If your customer has purchased X units of server/infrastructure and they are consuming 10% of their allocated units this month, then that is their Product activity score. You could track this score on a regular basis to make sure that you give timely notice to your customers when they are running out of hardware units and need to purchase more storage.

Depending on the nature of your products and your needs, you could make your product activity score as granular as you want it to be. For example, you can track usage of specific product features, customer behavior patterns and usage trends on specific days, times of year, and frequency to both improve your overall products and also to be able to react to risk indicators in a timely manner.

Customer Acquisition Cost (CAC)

Customer Acquisition Cost is a central guiding metric for marketing and sales. If the CAC is high, SaaS businesses struggle to recover their marketing and sales investments and attain a path to profitability.

Customer Success ROI

If CAC is a guiding metric for Marketing and Sales, what would be a similar guiding metric for Customer Success that would clearly encapsulate all post-sale activities, with a view toward establishing a return on investment thesis? To answer this question, we have to consider the following. In a post-sale/post-win operation, there are multiple phases of a customer's journey, like onboarding, adoption, expansion, and renewal that are impacted by differing serving functions like professional services, training, customer success, sales, and business development. Across these activities, there is a related collection of metrics that corresponds to particular phases – Time to Live (TTL) for onboarding, Adoption %, Customer Satisfaction (CSAT), NPS scores, Churn %, and so on. Some of these specific metrics are listed in Table 5-1.

Table 5-1. Customer Success ROI Metrics

ROI metrics	Description
Monthly recurring revenue (MRR)	Anticipated company income every month
Annual recurring revenue (ARR)	Anticipated company income every calendar year
Number of upsells	Upsells occur when customers purchase more of the same products/services they've already bought or other add-ons
Number of cross-sells	Customer purchases additional new products/services
Net promoter score	Score to determine customers' willingness to recommend the products/services of a company to others
Number of conversions	Number of customers who converted after trials to full-fledged customers
Number of renewals	No. of renewed contracts in a specific time period
Number of support tickets	Number of support tickets created by customers in a specific time period (engagement and satisfaction gauge)
Support tickets resolution time	Average time to resolve support tickets

CHAPTER 5   KEY METRICS AND BEYOND

While there doesn't appear to be an obvious unifying metric that aggregates across all the customer life cycle phases and touchpoints, a powerful proxy that we can employ to measure ongoing customer revenue contribution is **customer lifetime value (CLV/LTV)**. The impact of CLV can be measured and narrated at an MRR level. The greater the customer lifetime length (in months), the greater their value and profitability contribution through their lifetime. With regards to ROI, as investments are made in post-sale functions, ROI can be calculated based on the following formula:

Return on Investment (ROI) = (Net Program Benefits / Program Costs) * 100

In terms of Customer Success data:

Return on Investment (ROI) = ((Net Revenue Retention) / (Cost to Serve)) * 100

where Net Revenue Retention = $ARR (or $MRR) at start of period − $Churn + $Expansion; and, Cost to Serve = Aggregated cost of the post-sale operation.

Customer Success Guiding KPIs and Metrics

Table 5-2 shows a complete list of the relevant metrics and KPIs that should be tracked by your CS team, and your CS platform, if they are relevant to your business use case.

CHAPTER 5   KEY METRICS AND BEYOND

Table 5-2. *Customer Success Guiding KPIs and Metrics*

KPI	Description	Calculation	Success indicator
MRR	Anticipated company income every month	(Number of customers)*(avg. Billing per customer per month)	Amount increase
Net new MRR	Net MRR after accounting for churn, new subscriptions, and existing subscriptions' growth	New MRR + Expansion MRR – Churn MRR	Amount increase
Churn rate	% rate at which customers cancel recurring subscriptions	(Number of canceling customers for a time period)/(total Number of customers for that time period)*100	Rate increase
Retention rate	% of customers lost	[1 – (customers lost in a defined time period)/(total customers in that same time period)]*100	Rate increase
Revenue growth rate	Rate of Growth of MRR over previous month	[(Current MRR – Last Month's MRR)/Last Month's MRR]*100	Rate increase
Customer acquisition cost (CAC)	Cost of acquiring a customer	(Marketing + Sales Costs)/Number of new customers acquired	Amount increase
Customer lifetime value (CLV/LTV)	Prediction of net profits attributed to projected maximum customer growth	(Avg. MRR for customer)*(customer lifetime) where customer lifetime = 1/churn rate	Number increase

(*continued*)

Table 5-2. (*continued*)

KPI	Description	Calculation	Success indicator
LTV: CAC ratio	Lifetime value over customer acquisition cost	LTV/CAC	Higher than 3
Months to recover CAC	Duration before revenue from account cost of acquisition	CAC/Avg. MRR per customer	Less than 12 months
Inbound lead velocity	Rate at which qualified inbound leads are growing month over month	[(Number of leads in current month)/(Number of leads in prev. month)]*100	Rate increase

There is no dearth of material on how to measure the success and value of a Customer Success organization. But at the end of the day, you have to decide, as a CS leader or as a CS team member, which metrics are most valuable for your organization and for managing your customer portfolio. You need to know how those metrics relate to your company's success and your customers' success and experience and prioritize them accordingly.

Many of the metrics listed in the preceding are primarily focused on customer revenue, churn rate, lifetime value, and so on. If your Customer Success Organization encompasses Services, Support, Consulting, Training, etc., then the metrics to measure the effectiveness of those subfunctions would be different from the preceding.

For example, for your Services team, you will be measuring metrics like productive utilization (productive hours), billable utilization (billable hours), Annual Revenue per Billable Team Member, Profitability, Services ARR, Services NPS, and so on.

CHAPTER 5   KEY METRICS AND BEYOND

For your Support team, you will measure metrics like first response times to tickets, number of tickets grouped by prioritization, Ticket SLAs met %, number of total incidents in a defined time frame, number of escalations, root cause analysis, and Support NPS.

For Training, you would measure metrics like number of enrollments, average times to finish courses, Training CSAT, Enrollments to advanced courses, certifications, training enrollments/customer. Metrics that relate customer training and customer ROI are useful because better-trained customers deploy your products faster and better, resulting in faster time to value and better CSAT.

Based on the setup of your Customer Success Organization, its scope of functions and responsibility, the key metrics will have to be determined and captured accurately and then consolidated into usable dashboards based on your company profile, target audiences, and appetite and ability for automations and scale.

Once you have clarity on the different kinds of metrics you can capture, the next step is to group them as leading and lagging indicators for aiding your desired outcomes and for flagging risks. Next, we'll look at how to build a logical framework for effectively understanding leading and lagging indicators to incorporate into your overall customer health score. The following section has been written by Tom Lipscomb, a Bay Area executive who helps companies around the world deliver products and services that contribute to their Customers' Success.

Leading vs. Lagging Health/Churn Indicators

In this section, CS leader, Tom Lipscomb, discusses how you can group and leverage your leading and lagging risk and key performance indicators.

A leading indicator or KPI is a metric or statistic that is inherently predictive in nature, while a lagging indicator measures output that's already occurred to gain insight on future success.

There is a huge misconception that lagging metrics such as Revenue or Earnings are somehow "poor" KPIs. In reality, they are the most important ones. Unfortunately, when it comes to "what gets measured gets improved" they are a great starting point but are somewhat lacking in helping you to actually improve. The reason for this is the fact that they are lagging indicators. By the time you know what this year's (or quarter's) revenues and earnings are, it is too late to do anything about them.

If you look at the most commonly discussed Customer Success metrics, they are all actually quite useful, including Churn, Revenue Retention, Inbound Lead Velocity, and more. These are all great metrics that should be measured, tracked, and reported, but just recognize that they are inherently lagging.

Leading Indicators

A leading indicator or KPI is a metric or statistic that is inherently predictive in nature. As the Sleeter Group reports, "Leading Indicators tend to communicate change in the environment. They try to be predictive in nature."

So why do we focus so much on lagging metrics vs. the leading ones? Years ago, I had a colleague that made a great practical observation. She pointed out that part of the reason lagging indicators get used a lot is because they are easy to measure. We can pull them from Salesforce, or our financial systems. She also pointed out that although they can be easy to report on, they, in and of themselves, are hard to impact. At the same time, she suggested that leading indicators are different. Although they are much more useful to help us impact performance, they are harder to measure and tend to change over time.

CHAPTER 5   KEY METRICS AND BEYOND

If you take a look at the most commonly referenced KPIs, they are not only relatively easy to measure, they are generalizable, or relevant across a wide group of companies and industries. Unfortunately, leading indicators are not as easy to measure, and the ones you want to measure tend to be unique to you. As such, you don't see them discussed in the context of operationalization since they are hard to standardize and capture. For one thing, people will not typically agree upon the "magic ones" for good reasons. Their value is derived from the fact that they are aligned with how you run your business and execute on your strategies or address your challenges. There are exceptions, of course. Take NPS, which has as many detractors as promoters regarding its usefulness as a customer feedback tool. One of the strengths it does have is that it is promoted by many as a leading indicator of organic growth.

Secondly, NPS is generalizable. Virtually any company can ask the "ultimate question" about their business. Even Bain & Company states: "Net Promoter merely measures the quality of a company's relationships with its current customers, and high-quality relationships are a necessary, but insufficient, condition for profitable organic growth."

So what are the necessary and sufficient conditions for profitable growth? Of course, they include things like product market fit and minimally viable products. But they also include the ability to engage with customers in ways that support their success. This ultimately includes the processes and knowledge that are used to help your customers succeed; this is where process performance metrics come into play.

To understand these, let's take a look at an example of the logical decomposition of metrics, from lagging to leading to process performance. Figure 5-4 shows just such a framework, since things like pricing changes are not represented, but factors that affect tailwind (or headwind if you are actually lowering your pricing – ouch!) are.

CHAPTER 5 KEY METRICS AND BEYOND

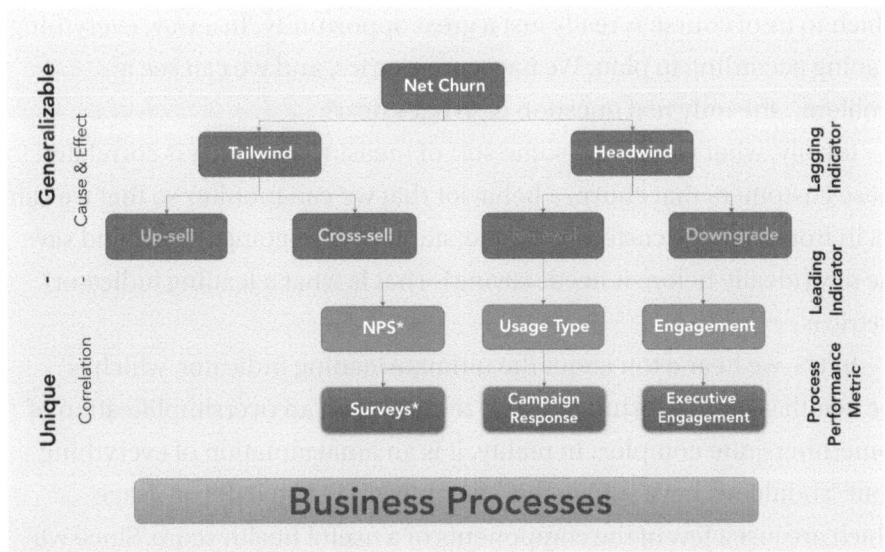

Figure 5-4. Framework for logical decomposition of metrics

Let's start by assuming that in the chart shown in Figure 5-4, we have a good net churn number – a negative one. Rather than use a negative (which is good) net churn (one vote for the negative net churn skeptics), we'll use a derivative of net churn, net revenue retention, because I like the intuitive, "we grew or shrank" view of the world!

Note Net revenue retention rate for a period = [[Start of period MRR + MRR from up-sell + MRR from price increases] − [MRR from churn + MRR from price decreases]] / [Start of period MRR].

Let's assume this number is 105% (growth), so at first glance, everything is pretty good, right? Well, that conclusion actually depends on your headwind vs. your tailwind. Let's assume that your headwind (downgrades and churned customers) is actually about 20%. When you look at the numbers this way, your investors think you have a problem,

105

which to us of course is really just a great opportunity. In a way, everything is going according to plan. We have our metrics, and we can see a problem...the only real question is: What's next?

Ideally, what we want is some sort of measurement that is correlated to those customers that churn, a behavior that we can monitor so that we can get in front of those customers, understand what is going wrong, and save the day (ideally before it needs saving). That is what a leading indicator/metric is.

In CS, we hear a ton about the ultimate leading indicator, which is the health score. Unfortunately, the term is often an oversimplification of something quite complex. In reality, it is an amalgamation of everything from "should we have sold to this customer?" (FIT) to NPS or Usage, which are just a few of the components of a useful health score. Since we are giving examples here, rather than an exhaustive list, let's just look at usage. Trust me, it's complicated enough. As for the example, let me share one I gathered while listening to a talk by the SVP of a publicly traded SaaS company (> $2B market cap). He commented that from a retention perspective, people storing files (usage type 1) is a good thing. But he also said that when multiple users access the same file (usage type 2), their stickiness (my words, not his) is much better. As such, assuming they've done some sort of correlation between their churning customers and usage type 2, they have a great leading indicator.

As much as this may be a really great example, as far as your business is concerned, this measurement may be (and probably is) totally meaningless. This is a reflection of the fact, stated earlier, that leading indicators tend to be more unique (vs. generalizable). Is this bad news? I don't think so. This is what makes the job of a Customer Success team great, and your company and customers unique. Figuring out your leading indicators (which change over time) is a critical part of how you add value as a team. Assuming you've already done this, or are up to the challenge, there is one more step. That step takes us to process performance metrics.

Process Performance Metrics

To continue with our example, even when we know that multiple people accessing the same file is a great leading indicator of long-term health and reduced churn, we have more to do. Our job includes figuring out how we are going to impact/increase/improve that leading indicator. Once again, referring to the preceding diagram, there are a number of ways in which we could impact this leading metric.

We could put a process in place to stress the value and simplicity of file sharing and collaboration during onboarding. This would be a process change. We would need to measure how many customers got the new training, and if their adoption of this capability is better than before the onboarding was changed. Basically, we can measure the process we put in place to drive our leading indicator. Another example could be to run an A/B campaign to inform existing customers, one in-app and the other via email. We could then understand which process (method) is effective (or if either of them are). The key here is to try to establish some correlation.

Ideally, this would be cause and effect, but having done this for years, this is often really hard to do. Establishing cause and effect is always tough, and is extremely challenging because in the real world, you usually take a multi-pronged approach. That doesn't mean, however, that you just wing it. At a minimum, you must measure if you are doing what you said you were going to do. If you are going to try to reach your customers with a campaign, you need to know you've reached 37% and establish if your approach has impacted your leading indicators/metrics. Then, for those who weren't reached by this method, you can systematically reach out to them by employing another approach and process (which should be measured as well).

This all sounds like a bunch of work, and of course, you could just play whack-a-mole, hoping to get lucky. If, on the other hand, you prefer to be great, consider how the information shared here can be used to drive your company to even greater heights. Remember, this isn't just the sort of thing big companies do; this is what little companies do to become big companies.

CHAPTER 5   KEY METRICS AND BEYOND

Now that we have a clear understanding of how to leverage leading and lagging indicators to measure performance and risks, let us now look at some key metrics depending on the stage of the company.

Examples of Quantitative Metrics Based on Company or Customer Journey Stage

Table 5-3. *Metrics Based on Company Stage*

Early-stage startups 0–25MM ARR	Mid-late stage startups 25–100MM ARR	Enterprise/public companies > 100MM ARR

• Customer Onboarding Process
  ○ Onboarding time
  ○ First time to value
• Initial Contract Value
• CSAT
• Support tickets resolution times
	All metrics on the left plus:
	• Retention Rate
	• YoY growth rate
	• Churn rate
	• CAC
	• ARR/NRR
	• Customer Perceived Value
	• NPS
		All metrics on the left plus:
		• Near real-time health score
		• Engagement score
		• CLV Progression
		• VoC

Table 5-3 shows some of the metrics that are important to capture based on the stage of your company. While this is not an all-inclusive list, it should give you a good starting point for your analytical modeling and reporting exercises. Similarly, let's look at an example of a Customer Journey map that also contains associated metrics for each phase (Figure 5-5).

CHAPTER 5 KEY METRICS AND BEYOND

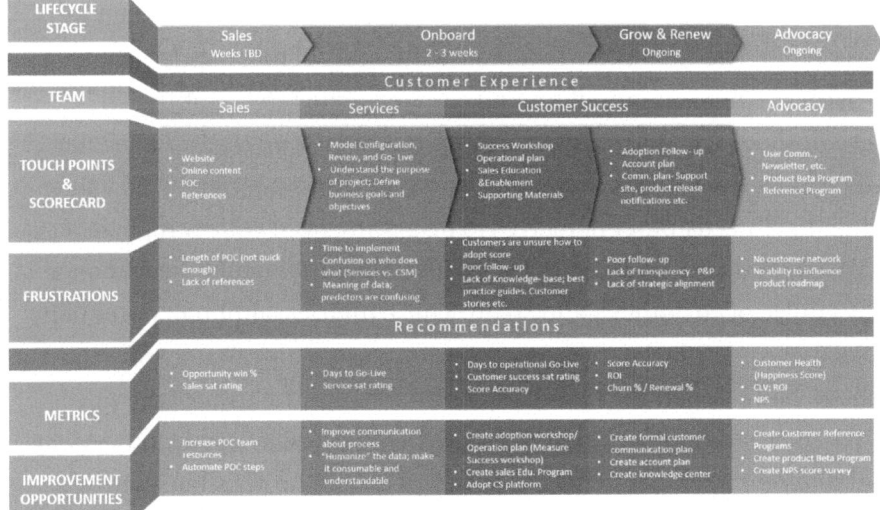

Figure 5-5. Example of expanded Customer Journey map with metrics

Once you've identified the metrics that your company needs, the next question is how do you capture these metrics?

Capturing Quantitative Metrics

Capturing some of the metrics like contract value and ARR can be easily done based on signed customer contracts and revenue predictors based on sales pipeline and forecasting. Capturing usage and adoption-based metrics could be trickier depending on the type of product.

For pure SaaS products, capturing usage metrics might be easier if the customers have to log onto your systems to take actions and engage. For products that are on customer premises and not on cloud (on-prem), capturing usage metrics might be dependent on customers sharing their usage information with you. So you have to identify creative ways to get their usage data by doing performance reviews and system health checks or using other means. Clearly articulating the value to the customer of sharing that data with you will increase the odds of that happening.

With partners and resellers, you can negotiate terms upfront so they will share their end customers and usage information on a regular basis. Some of the metrics are qualitative like customer perceived value (value that the customer perceives to be getting from your company and products), CSAT feedback, qualitative customer health (based on a CSM's pulse of customer), and so on. These metrics, although potentially subjective, are critical to provide a view into a customer's state of mind and point of view, something that the quantifiable metrics cannot provide.

An ideal situation is a system where the metrics flow in automatically from different systems. While this may not always be possible, getting as close as possible to such a system should be the goal of any Customer Success Operations practice that supports a Customer Success Organization.

We've spent a lot of time talking about systems-driven quantitative metrics for a company and Customer Success organization. Adopting a customer-centric approach, let us now focus on how to identify and co-define outcomes-driven KPIs and metrics jointly with your customer.

CHAPTER 5   KEY METRICS AND BEYOND

Thinking Beyond Numbers – Co-defining Outcomes and KPIs

Back to the Basics

While there are many organizations and executives who are completely driven by quantifiable data and swear by it, it is very important to understand that the success of your customers is driven by criteria beyond just the adoption, usage, and revenue data that you capture. The backbone of all things Customer Success is about understanding the following:

- Why did the customer purchase your product?
- What is the problem they are trying to solve?
- Are they able to solve it after purchasing your product?

- How quickly are they able to do it?
- What does success mean to them?
- Do they see value in purchasing your product?
- If yes, how much value do they see?
- If they don't see value, why not?
- How do customers rate their experience with your company and products?

These are basic questions that need to be answered with confidence and accuracy, before you even think about growth, expansion, and long-term partnerships with that customer. The answers you get can be converted into qualitative account metrics. You need to talk to customers directly and regularly to understand a lot of this information. And THAT is irreplaceable.

Co-defining Customer KPIs

The best way to identify the right KPIs for measuring your customers' success is to co-define those KPIs with them. Onboarding is the best phase to establish benchmark KPIs based on your customers' desired outcomes. The best way to do that is to do your homework and study your customers' business before discussing their KPIs with them. Always make sure to review the defined metrics and KPIs on a quarterly basis with the customer to verify accuracy and relevancy. Co-define the KPIs and have the customer take joint ownership to hit the KPIs by taking responsibility for their tasks. This also helps lower the risks. And last but not least, establish clear desired outcomes and measurement so you can track and report the KPIs effectively.

For example, one of us was working with a retail customer with an online sales portal and app that were powered by our platform. Our initial assumption was that the customer's primary success criteria would be the volume of sales generated by the online portal and app. Upon validating with the customer, we found out that while the online sales were important, they measured the success of online assets through the volumes and ratings of their user reviews. That was the key criteria for them, since the user reviews impacted their overall reputation as they were transitioning to an online and app-based model. We would never have known this without validating their KPIs with them. Armed with this information, we were able to capture the right metrics to clearly articulate the customer's expected ROI.

In addition to quantitative metrics, outcomes-driven qualitative metrics also play a key role in building a robust customer ROI strategy.

Outcomes-Driven Qualitative Metrics

Outcomes-driven qualitative metrics are a core component of your CS Operations strategy. Will they be as easy to define and measure as the quantitative metrics? Absolutely not. Will you be able to fully automate the collection and analysis of these metrics? Likely not; unless they are being collected by/from robots, that is. Is it easy to collect these metrics? It depends. It depends on the relationship you have with the customer. It depends on if they think of you as a trusted advisor and are comfortable sharing their honest thoughts with you about your products, how they are using them and even how they are not using them and how you might be losing out to the competition.

Table 5-4 shows a sampling of the qualitative metrics that you should be capturing and building into your overall customer health, engagement, and value assessments and scores.

Table 5-4. *CS Qualitative Metrics*

Metric	Description
Customer Use Cases	Clear understanding of the use cases where the customer is using your products
Desired Outcomes	What are the customers' desired outcomes?
Success Criteria	What are their success criteria for them? Both how they will measure your company's value and how their own success is measured
Major Milestones (identified and progression tracking)	Major milestones/checkpoints leading to desired outcomes
Total Time to Onboard	How long it took to onboard the customer?
Time from Onboarding to First Time to Value	How long it took for the customer to start seeing value from using your products and services?
Which other products is the customer required to use along with your products to fulfill their desired outcomes and success criteria?	List all the complementary and supplementary products here
Customer Sentiment	(Red/Yellow/Green)–- Red flag should create immediate action triggers
CSAT/NPS Qualitative Feedback	Qualitative Feedback captured from the customer
Onboarding Time	Total time it took to onboard the customer (ends with customer sign-off of the onboarding completion)
Onboarding Major Milestones time	Broken down by each milestone

(*continued*)

Table 5-4. (*continued*)

Metric	Description
Customer Perceived Value	1–5 rating with 5 being 100%+ value to 1 being 0%
Your footprint in the company	Total no. of use cases or applications that can use your products/no. of use cases that are using your products
Are your products part of the customer's standard stack (approved by their internal teams for broad usage)?	Y/N

Capturing Qualitative Metrics

You can collect qualitative metrics in a number of different ways. For example, through manual formal touchpoints, informal water cooler conversations, during strategic business reviews, and by engaging with your customer stakeholders at all levels and picking their brains about what they are up to and what is important to them. Table 5-5 articulates some of the best practices to follow when quizzing customers about their KPIs and metrics.

Table 5-5. *Best Practices to Collect CS Qualitative Metrics*

	Push Customers out of their comfort zone. Make sure that they fully comprehend the importance of the data/metrics they desire and are also clear on how to capture those metrics.
	Challenge the Objectives • Is it really important or just nice to have? • What's the impact and priority?
	Challenge the Metrics Are they clear and measurable? • "I want my test processes to become simpler." vs. • "I want manual intervention in my test processes to be reduced to < 20%."
 vs. 	Metrics vs. KPIs • Make sure that customer understands the difference between the metrics and KPIs. • Question the customer regarding the group/function and personal objectives. • Help the customer define the KPIs measuring the objectives. • Gather the industry benchmark data for KPIs.

Once you go through all this effort of building the relationships, spending time with the customers, and collecting all the qualitative metrics, will they be useful? Well, if applied properly and when used in conjunction with the quantifiable metrics, they can be a potential goldmine. They can help you take a clear and accurate customer pulse by helping you understand the "Customer Perceived Value" (CPV). CPV helps you measure customer loyalty and long-term customer partnerships. It has traditionally been a marketing metric that can and should be applied as a key metric of a Customer Success org.

Customer Perceived Value (CPV)

As shown in Figure 5-6, the Customer Success Org. plays a very important role in creating life-long customers and strengthening customer loyalty and relationships. The Customer Perceived Value (CPV) plays a starring role in this regard by helping measure the value that a customer perceives to be getting from a company overall, not just through the usage of their products.

CPV could be less or more than the "quantifiable Value/ROI" that a company provides to a customer, since it is driven by the customer's perception of the value they are getting. CPV is not easy to measure and typically strengthens over time, playing a critical role in ensuring customer loyalty, especially when things are not going well.

In our early days in Customer Success, one of our customers was a retail giant with an online sales portal powered by our company. December was their busiest time of the year for online sales. One December, our company's platform crashed, bringing down the customer's online portal for more than 48 hours and causing significant loss of both revenue and reputation (user ratings). Needless to say, the ROI/value that the company got by using our platform nose-dived in that period.

Our Customer Success Manager for that customer took responsibility and proactively worked with them on actionable mitigation paths, looping in our executive team into customer conversations so that the customer knew we understood their pain at the highest level. The result was that, once the issue was fixed, one of the customer's senior leaders told our CSM not to worry and that we'd get through the situation together. Despite the losses, the company stayed with us as a loyal customer and gave us an average NPS score of 9 immediately following this debacle.

CHAPTER 5 KEY METRICS AND BEYOND

Figure 5-6. *Role of Customer Success in creating life-long customers*

The Customer Success and Services Teams; in particular the Account, Delivery, and Customer Success Managers, play a significant role in building and strengthening CPV. If your CPV is positive, ideally customers'' perception of your company as a trusted partner stay stable, even if the actual value goes down temporarily because of an outage or other issues for which the customer might hold your company responsible.

CHAPTER 5 KEY METRICS AND BEYOND

How to Calculate Customer Perceived Value?

While Marketing organizations use a formula like total value–total cost to calculate CPV, from a CS perspective, you will have to derive CPV based on multiple discussions with customers to understand their usage, perceived value, and ROI from their investment in your company and products. That is why we are classifying CPV as a qualitative metric vs. a quantitative one.

You could use a qualitative gauge to measure your customer's CPV. Either something like red, yellow, green or ratings of 1–5, with 1 being very bad and 5 very good. The Customer Success Managers should enter this value in the CS systems based on their understanding of the account and the customer's sentiment.

CPV is a metric that can either strengthen or weaken over time based on CX, customers' feelings toward your company, and so on. It is also an individualistic metric, that is, the CPV of every individual customer stakeholder could be different based on whether they like working with you or not. In some cases, their CPV might have no relation to the kind of experience you might be providing them. For example, if the customer stakeholder prefers a competitor's product because they have used it more or have some other underlying reason, you might not be able to do much to influence their feelings.

However, it is important to note and track CPV to identify your company's champions and detractors beyond the baseline NPS scores so that you can both leverage your champions as needed and work with your current detractors to improve their perception. Monitoring and tracking CPV also gives you greater predictability of churn and escalations management when things are not going well with the customer. A high CPV usually increases the chances of a customer sticking with you, through thick and thin, with significantly reduced risk of churn even if there could be a decrease in their ROI from your products due to temporary issues like outages or bugs.

CHAPTER 5   KEY METRICS AND BEYOND

A close, collaborative relationship between buyers and suppliers was traditionally found in Japan. Known as *keiretsu*, this business philosophy was the subject of a 2013 article in *Harvard Business Review* by Katsuki Aoki and Thomas Taro Lennerfors. Keiretsu lost some of its luster during the cost-cutting of the 1990s but is now being revived and reinvented. The article revealed that some of Japan's most dominant companies had quietly been turning their supplier relationships into a tool to help them innovate faster while also radically cutting costs.

Toyota provides a compelling example. Today, the company has vendor relationships that are more open, more global, and more cost-conscious than traditional keiretsu ever were. They provide even stronger bonds of trust, cooperation, and educational support. The authors examined the evolution of Toyota's keiretsu and the numerous lessons for developed-world and emerging-market companies seeking to improve their supplier relationships for lasting gain.

In summary, such companies should think short-term and long-term; know their suppliers well and develop trust with them; balance implicit and explicit communication; identify the suppliers most worth improving; and involve suppliers in developing new products. Although the article focused on strong supplier relationships, similar bonds of trust, cooperation, and support can be formed with customers to promote long-term brand loyalty and trust.

In this chapter, we reviewed the key metrics for measuring the effectiveness of a Customer Success organization. We also reviewed common CS KPIs and related metrics, both qualitative and quantitative, that it is important to capture as part of the customer's lifecycle and discussed their grouping into leading and lagging indicators.

CHAPTER 5   KEY METRICS AND BEYOND

What lessons can we apply to the Customer Success executives at the beginning of this chapter, one of whom has access to too many data points and the second who was building her CS Org from scratch? The solution for both is that they can zero-in on the key qualitative and quantitative metrics and KPIs by mapping them directly to the Customer Success Organizational Value.

The next logical question is, how do you use Customer Success metrics and KPIs? What should you do with the data you captured and what kinds of dashboards should you build? We will answer these questions in the next chapter.

CHAPTER 6

Making Sense of Data

One of our customers had two models in its product range; a regular model and a premium model. The main differentiating feature of the premium model, which cost more, was its support of a mobile app. Consumers could use the app to control the product, including features like setting timers remotely.

To find out how consumers were actually using the premium product, we tracked usage analytics via dashboards. And it was during one routine check of the health dashboard that our Customer Success Manager (CSM) made a discovery. Despite high sales of the product, usage of the mobile app-based features were very low. This was a risk to the sales and ROI of the premium model since the mobile app was the key differentiating feature.

Our CSM brought this issue to the customer's notice and after further research, the customer discovered the source of the problem. The product packaging did not highlight the premium features properly, leaving consumers either unaware of their existence or their value. When the issue was corrected, the data immediately reflected a positive change of behavior and adoption of the premium features, resulting in a grateful and happy customer.

This example shows that collecting and visualizing data can be used to track risks and deliver the desired results. But while you could be collecting a lot of data about your customers and overall CS practice, it needs to be processed, visualized, and presented in the right manner for easy consumption and analysis. If not, its value and usability reduces significantly. Remember, data is not information. Data needs to be processed and presented properly to become usable information.

Typically, one of the first things Customer Success leaders do when they start, or inherit, a Customer Success practice is to review existing customer insights dashboards to determine value and gaps. In this chapter, we will look at the different ways in which key metrics captured through listening posts deployed throughout the customer journey can be visualized via reports and dashboards. By doing so, a CS practice can capture the desired results and business intelligence it needs to function effectively. The dashboards would be built and maintained by the Customer Success Center of Excellence.

Once you collect your key metrics, both qualitative and quantitative, the next logical step is to think about how best to use those metrics to do the following:

- Create views and dashboards for different audiences to quickly access the information they need.

- Consolidate metrics from different sources to create a 360-degree view of the customer.

- Identify opportunities for improving operational efficiencies through repeatable processes and targeted actions tied to the captured metrics.

- Identify opportunities for automation (auto analysis of data and triggers for action) and scaling processes using the captured metrics.

By having a set of data that's personalized and targeted to them, a department head is not overwhelmed by unnecessary data. The Head of Sales, for example, can immediately see how sales this quarter compare to the same period last year. Similarly, based on a 360-degree view of the customer, the Head of CS gets real-time insights into how key metrics like consumption, ARR, and growth are trending over a certain time period and is able to do accurate forecasting.

CS Managers and CSMs can monitor customer health and status dashboards for their portfolio accounts on a regular basis and use the derived intelligence in their internal and customer business reviews. By building learning and pattern-recognition models into your data visualization techniques, you can quickly identify areas of improvement and/or risk, both for yourself and your customers. However, none of this data will be useful unless you know what you want to get out of it.

What Are Your Desired Outcomes?

Have you identified your customer's desired outcomes and success criteria? Have you done that for all your customers to identify patterns and trends? Great! Now it's time to think about your own desired outcomes and success criteria. Your own organizational and team members' criteria are equally important to understand and capture. This will allow you, your team, and cross-functional stakeholders to get access to the right information at the right time in order to make the critical decisions needed to maximize your customers' success as well as your company's success.

For example, if one of your desired outcomes is fast and timely renewal cycles, you could have dashboards to monitor upcoming renewals and/or services consumption. Data-driven triggers would alert the sales and customer success teams about the optimum time to initiate renewal, upsell, or expansion discussions with customers based on your service's consumption patterns.

Equally, if you want to reduce overall customer onboarding time, you can have triggers set to identify onboarding outliers or risks and tie them to specific actions, either manual or automated. For example, if a customer is stuck on a particular onboarding step for too long, it could be a cause for concern. An automated help email could be fired by the system to provide additional assistance for that step. A manual risk flag can also be raised with the account's Customer Success Manager for manual follow-up as needed.

Once you know your desired outcomes, the next logical question is how to map them to the right metrics.

How to Map Metrics to Desired Outcomes

Some of the common desired outcomes for a company, irrespective of size, are good customer health, steady or increasing customer recurring revenue and growth, customer loyalty, and brand consolidation.

Let's now map these desired outcomes to metrics, as shown in Table 6-1.

Table 6-1. Mapping Desired Outcomes to Metrics

Desired outcome	Metrics
Customer health	Adoption rate per customer, engagement per customer, no. of years they've been a customer, growth trends
Steady or increasing ARR and customer growth	Increasing no. of customers, increasing ARR per customer, YoY growth per customer, growth forecasting, services consumption forecasting
Customer experience and loyalty	NPS, CSAT, high Customer Perceived Value per customer, new leads from customers, increased customer participation in customer advisory boards and company conferences
Brand consolidation	Referenceable big brand customers, increasing market footprint, industry awards, and positive PR

Once you know the metrics you need to collect to achieve your desired outcomes, it's time to build a reusable customer data model to capture and consolidate customer information in a standardized and unified manner.

CHAPTER 6   MAKING SENSE OF DATA

A company-wide standard and unified customer data model is the backbone of any CS system that is built for scale and automation. The data model allows you to identify and map customer information in a consistent way, irrespective of the systems the information resides in. For example, defining a standard customer data model within your company where a distinct Customer ID is mapped to a customer, company-wide, irrespective of which tool or department the customer data resides in, makes it easier to collect and map relevant information to that customer holistically.

Irrespective of whether you are using a CRM tool, a Customer Success tool, a Support tool or a combination of tools to manage your customer data; when the time comes to consolidate customer information and build a customer 360 dashboard, it becomes easy because of the underlying standardized customer data model.

Imagine the pain of doing this exercise if each tool/department had its own unique customer identifier and customer data model. Stitching the customer information together to get the full picture of customer engagement and health would become a nightmare.

We will explore some of the CS data modeling design best practices and examples in Chapter 7. The CS data model is the stepping stone to map your metrics to desired outcomes, both customers' and your own, to build a holistic customer 360 dashboard. A Customer 360 dashboard provides a consolidated view of a customer, including but not limited to current contracts info, ARR, consumption trends, support tickets, success plans. major milestones, and more.

Building a Customer 360 Dashboard

In this section, Senior CS Executive and SVP of Global Customer Success & Support, Dev Kurbur, discusses the important components to build a comprehensive customer 360 dashboard.

CHAPTER 6   MAKING SENSE OF DATA

If you are a Head of Customer Success, your main objective is maximize your customers desired business outcomes and experience by using your products and services to maximize retention and growth. Easier said than done, right? So, how do you ensure the customer's success, the success of your CS practice and the success of your company?

Well, it is not possible to accomplish this objective by focusing on customer health KPIs alone. Instead, it is imperative to have customer 360 dashboards and tools consisting of different components that show you what is going on with your customers at all times, as shown in Figure 6-1.

The first component of a customer 360 dashboard should be comprehensive customer health indicators split into external and internal views depending on the level of detail in your data collection. The second component is company-wide KPIs so that particular efforts and campaigns can be quantified and tracked. The third component is a set of KPIs that enable heads of CS to measure the performance of their own teams and practice, since most also have a functional responsibility toward post-sales, customer-facing functions.

A common team KPI system will encourage standardization of best practices and foster a sense of clarity and camaraderie since team members are all striving toward similar goals. The key is to keep your KPIs simple, consistent, and well-defined. An effective dashboard, when developed correctly, will allow for easy interpretation and communication within the organization.

Figure 6-1. *Customer 360 dashboard components*

Customer Health Indicators

Customer Health is the primary indicator of the strength of the business relationship. A dashboard equipped with accurate health trackers will be able to monitor customer sentiment and usage and provide accurate churn updates. It is the job of your CS team to determine which factors should be tracked, and which will provide true insight into the health of a customer.

Some factors to consider:

- Solution and Impact – Are you really solving the customer's problems?

- Value and ROI – Is the customer ROI better than if the customer did it in-house or with a competitor?

- Friction – How much effort does the customer have to expend to get what they need when using your products and services

Company-wide KPIs

Company-wide KPIs allow you to track your customers in real time and answer key questions that have to do with their business status. Are other functional areas moving the customers in their journey? Are there any bottlenecks? Do they need any help? Are you helping them hit their KPIs?

Every department in an organization, whether they know it or not, interfaces directly or indirectly with customers. It is the CS team's job to make sure each one is focused on delivering real value to customers and continually optimizes the delivery. It's important to measure this process and provide full transparency for all relevant stakeholders to promote an accurate understanding of where things stand at all times. It is important to keep track of company-wide KPIs like

- Customer retention rates: churn rates; customer loss analysis data – why are they leaving?
- Upsell and cross-sell metrics.
- Lifetime value of customer (LTV).
- Product adoption and usage.
- Bugs and enhancement requests.
- NPS and customer satisfaction scores.

Customer Success KPIs

Customer Success Team KPIs are an internal measure of how your team is performing in relation to team goals. How well are you meeting your customers' needs? How are you performing in terms of contributing to customer happiness? Which practices are effective? Who are your star performers? Who needs improvement, and why?

Keeping track of these metrics will allow you to discard practices that aren't effective, and test new ones for their efficacy. In the same fashion, team turnover will allow you to find the successful team members and utilize their strategies as team best practices.

Most CS teams have three branches: Onboarding and Training, Support, and Customer Success Management. Here are some of their responsibilities and the metrics they track:

- Onboarding
    - Time to first customer value
    - Activation rate
    - Onboarding costs and timelines
    - Onboarding customer transactional survey

- Support
  - Traditional metrics for service such as time to respond, wait times, time to resolve, support costs, satisfaction surveys
- Customer Success team
  - Value delivery
  - Adoption and usage rates
  - Relationship status with customers
  - Proactive CSM activity
  - Value to the company – retention rates, upsell/cross-sell, customer advocacy
  - Value to other teams inside company – provide feedback, bug testing, advice
  - Cost of Customer Success team vs. revenue increases because of their efforts

These three factors: the Customer Health Indicators, Customer KPIs and CS Team KPIs, are the most critical features of a Customer Success dashboard. This trifecta ensures your customers' needs are met and your team is able to perform their jobs with the most efficacy. A customer 360 dashboard equips your Head of Customer Success with the necessary tools for achieving Customer Success from the inside out.

CHAPTER 6   MAKING SENSE OF DATA

Key Features of a Customer Success 360 Tool

So far, we've discussed the customer health data and KPIs that your customer 360 dashboard should incorporate. When you're looking to purchase a customer success tool for your CS practice or build one in-house, there are certain key features that you would need to ensure that the right data integration, dashboarding, and communication capabilities are supported. At a minimum, a robust customer success tool and 360 system should be able to do the following:

- Provide a unified view of customer data.
- Integrate data sources quickly and easily.
- Automate customer workflows.
- Support advanced customer segmentation.
- Provide reports exporting capabilities.
- Support streamlined customer communications.

Let us now take a look at each one of these features in more detail.

Unified View of Customer Data

The goal of building a customer 360 dashboard is to have **a single, unified system of record for each and every customer**, as shown in Figure 6-2. Customer information can be pulled into a single dashboard from disparate systems as needed. Real-time health scoring will help identify key customers' statuses and alert you to critical status changes.

CHAPTER 6 MAKING SENSE OF DATA

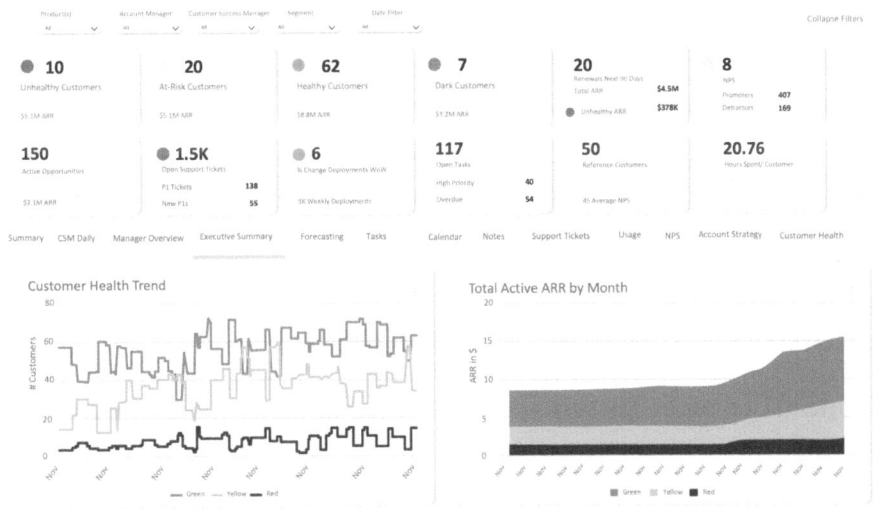

Figure 6-2. *Unified customer data view*

Integrate Data Sources Swiftly and Easily

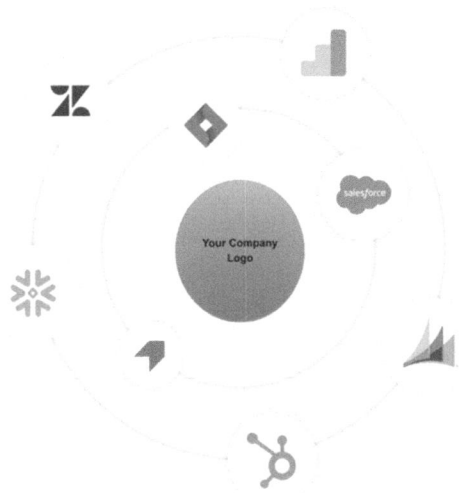

Figure 6-3. *Customer data integration*

CHAPTER 6   MAKING SENSE OF DATA

Your customer 360 system should provide and support mechanisms to ensure swift onboarding and connections to other systems. Like, providing a library of API-based connectors. Ingestion of data from non-standard sources should also be supported. Figure 6-3 shows a sample data integration ecosystem with varied data sources like Salesforce (CRM data), Hubspot (CRM), Snowflake (Ops data), Zendesk (Support data), etc.

Automate Customer Workflows

Advanced Customer 360 systems and CS tools should support the creation and deployment of simple, visual, and powerful trigger- and action-based workflows to efficiently target customer groups and trigger relevant actions, as shown in Figure 6-4. You should be able to streamline your daily operations with tasks, playbooks, and outreach triggers that are truly automated. We will look at automations more closely in Chapter 7.

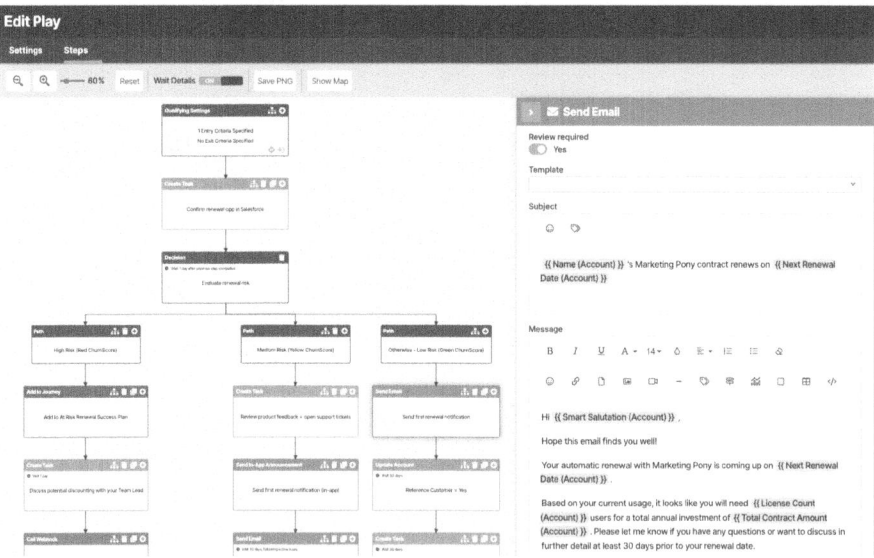

Figure 6-4. Customer workflows automation

CHAPTER 6 MAKING SENSE OF DATA

Support Advanced Customer Segmentation

A Customer 360 system should support the creation of specialized customer segments dashboards based on customer attributes such as profitability, geography, verticals, utilization or consumption, and much more. This provides valuable context and a granular view when you are looking to derive actionable insights to meet your desired business outcomes. Customer segments, as shown in Figure 6-5, can be utilized in customer health scoring, dashboard reporting, task delegation, and workflows automations.

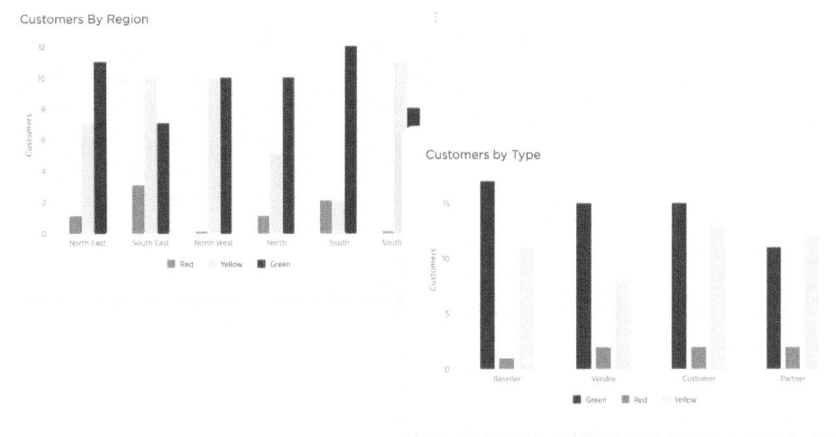

Figure 6-5. Customer segmentation dashboards

Support Report Exporting Capabilities

A CS tool should support the export of relevant data from your customer 360 systems in PDF, PPT, Word, XLS, and other report formats for customer-facing and internal business reviews and other reporting needs (Figure 6-6). Reports should incorporate your own logo-branded templates and be automatically scheduled to be sent out.

CHAPTER 6   MAKING SENSE OF DATA

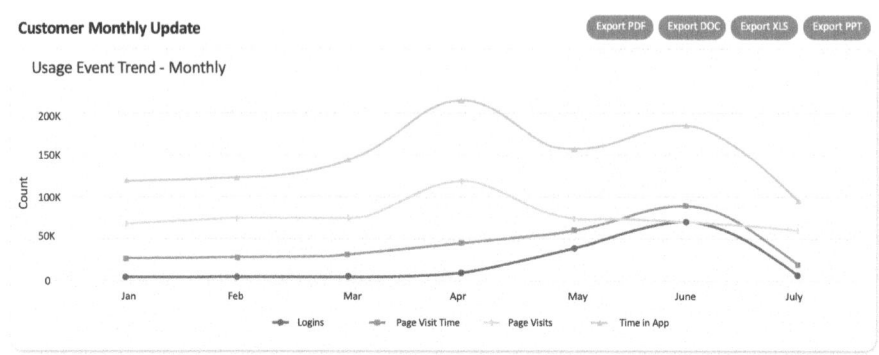

Figure 6-6. Exporting customer reports

Support Streamlined Customer Communication

A customer 360 system should enable you to send surveys and emails to customers, as shown in Figure 6-7. Emails can be templated with merge fields and personalized as needed.

Subject	Status	Issue Report Date	Next Steps
Missing device data	New	Nov 10, 2022	Internal review with technical team to determine issue
System status screen not refreshing properly	Pending	Oct 30, 2022	Awaiting customer to confirm on bug fix QA
Fixes in software version 2.5	Closed	Oct 27, 2022	Information sent to customer
System crash	Pending	Oct 14, 2022	Awaiting additional information from customer
Performance inadequate for third consecutive week	Pending	Sep 20, 2022	Awaiting customer to confirm bug fix QA
User not found error	Open	Sep 15, 2022	Should be updated in next software release
Signal panel shuts down intermittently	New	Sep 01, 2022	Cannot reproduce. Technical team is debugging
'Get User Activity History' documentation missing	Closed	Aug 10, 2022	Documentation Updated

Figure 6-7. Customer communication dashboard

CHAPTER 6 MAKING SENSE OF DATA

Let's now look at some sample dashboards that CS executives, managers, and CSMs can use to effectively track the desired business outcomes for their CS practices.

Sample Dashboards

Executive Dashboards

The executive dashboards are for senior leaders to keep track of the overall health of the Customer Success practice. They have a key focus on ARR/NRR, billing and expansion trends, and growth forecasting. Figure 6-8 shows a template for an executive dashboard for a mature CS practice with multiple regions, industry verticals, and contract types. The dashboard shows KPIs at region and country levels and year over year (YoY) performance overview by region and customer segments.

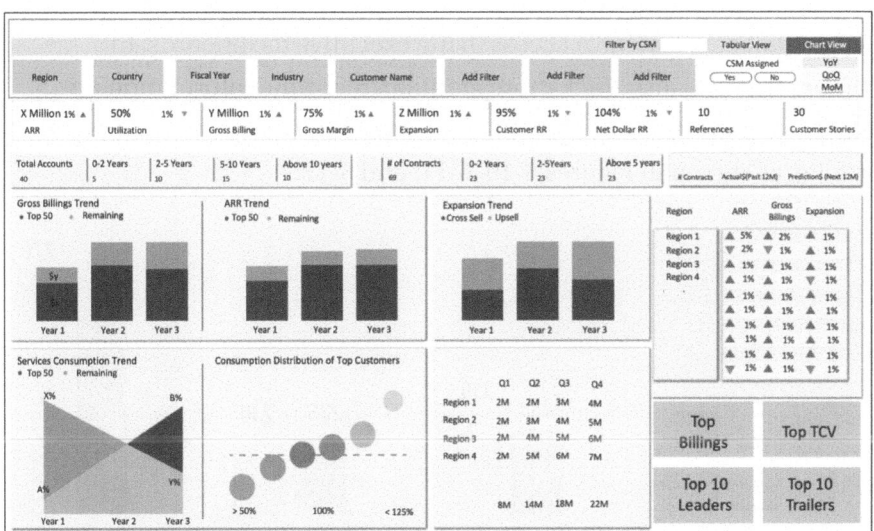

Figure 6-8. Executive dashboard

CHAPTER 6 MAKING SENSE OF DATA

Figure 6-9 shows a CS KPI snapshot with the ability to compare KPIs between CS covered and non-covered accounts. You can tweak the filters to add and remove as needed to make the comparison more useful for you. Having a view like this would allow a CS leader to show the ROI from Customer Success-covered accounts and make a case for CS growth.

	Active Customers	ARR Growth	Adoption Growth	Gross Billings Growth	Expansion Growth Upsell	Expansion Growth Cross Sell	Expansion Growth Overall
CSM Covered		< show in red if negative> <show in green if positive>					
Non CSM Covered							

Figure 6-9. *CS KPI overview*

Manager Dashboards

The CS Managers can have access to the executive dashboards. In addition, they can also track more granular, real-time information on budgets, actuals, customer health, and churn indicators for their specific portfolio, as shown in Figures 6-10, 6-11, and 6-12.

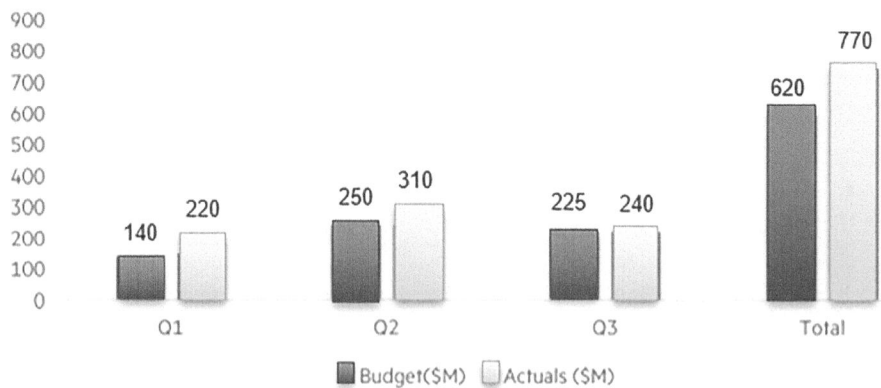

Figure 6-10. *QoQ CS budgets vs. actuals performance overview – bookings*

138

CHAPTER 6   MAKING SENSE OF DATA

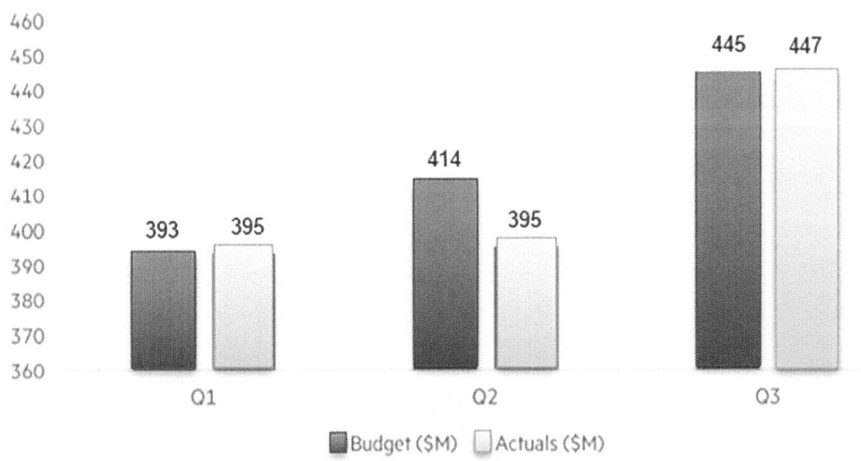

Figure 6-11. *QoQ CS budgets vs. actuals performance overview – ARR*

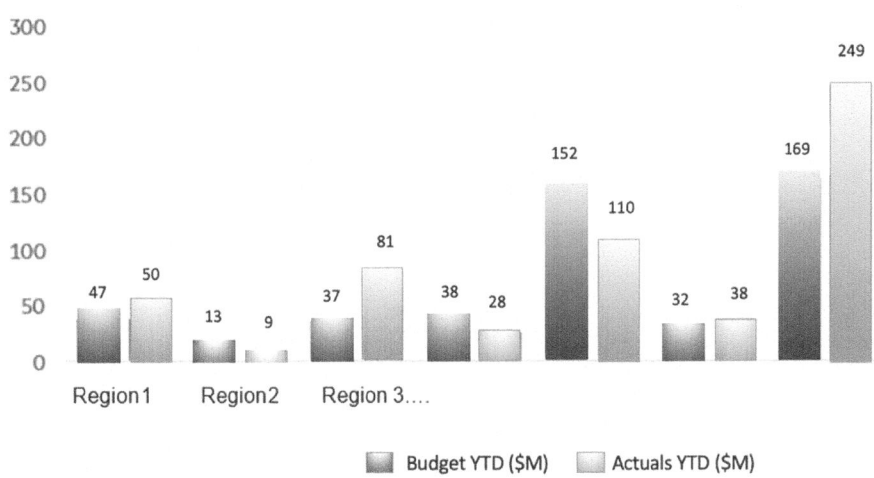

Figure 6-12. *CS budgets vs. actuals performance – regional drill-down (YTD)*

139

CHAPTER 6   MAKING SENSE OF DATA

Figures 6-13 and 6-14 show views that track consolidated onboarding and customer health information for easy analysis and reporting.

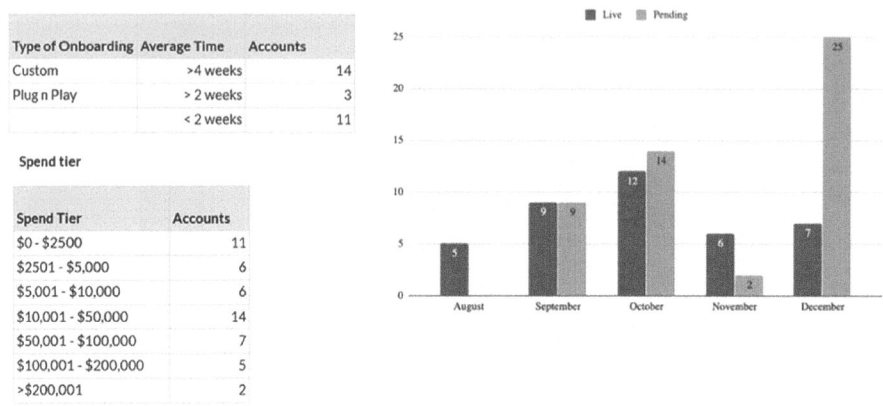

Figure 6-13.   Customer onboarding review dashboard

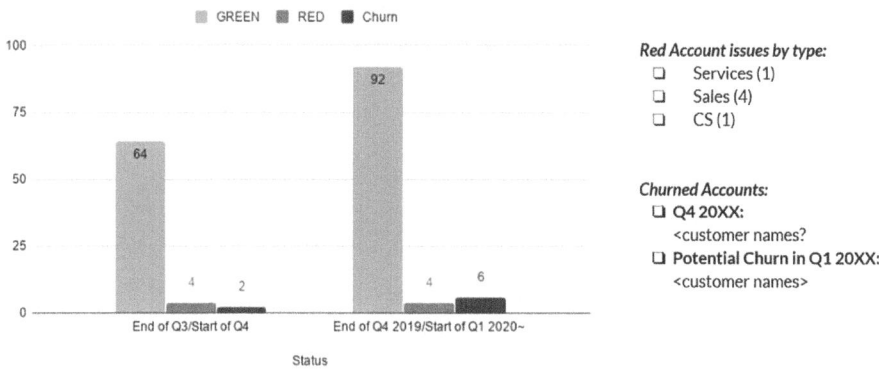

Figure 6-14.   Customer health review dashboard

CSM Dashboards

CSM dashboards provide useful views of a CSM's account portfolio. Information about customer accounts' health, performance, success plans, calls to action, communications with the customer, upcoming calls to action, and related day-to-day activities. Table 6-2 shows a detailed view

CHAPTER 6 MAKING SENSE OF DATA

of a sample CSM account and Table 6-3 a sample list view. These types of views should be built within the primary Customer Success tool and customer 360 system that the CSM uses on a day-to-day basis.

Table 6-2. CSM Account View

ROW 1: Label and input field	ROW 2: Label and input field
Onboarding Type <New/Upsell>	Implementation Stage: <Pre-Onboarding, Onboarding, Blocked by Product, Blocked by CS, Blocked by PubOps, Blocked by Sales, Onboarding On Track, Live> – drop down
Primary Customer Contact <pull list from SFDC contacts?>	Last Contacted Date
Engagement: High Touch/Low Touch – Drop down	Sales-CS handoff date
Customer Success Manager – drop down	PreOnboarding call date
AdOps – drop down list (optional)	Onboarding call date
Customer Health: red/yellow/green – dropdown	Publishers Live Date
Health reason: Text area – required to be filled if customer is red or yellow	Go Live ETA date
Executive Summary	Go Live Actual date

(*continued*)

Table 6-2. (*continued*)

ROW 1: Label and input field	ROW 2: Label and input field	
Executive Summary Archive	Days to go live (difference between onboarding call date and Go Live Actual date) – to be calculated automatically	
Current Month Spend/TV Projection: Free text for now	Agency (activated only if New Instance is N)	
Account Created (Y/N)	Notes (Add Onboarding blockers info here)	
New Instance (Y/N). If N then	Business Opportunities/Risks	
Related JIRAs – text area	Call to Actions (CTAs)	Link to CTAs

Table 6-3. CSM Account List View

Customer name	Current stage	Next milestone	Health	Success plan	Calls to action	Renewal Date
Cust 1	Onboarding	Onboarding call	Green	\<link to success plan\>	\<link to customer CTAs\>	
Cust 2	Growth	Business review				

Table 6-4 shows the prioritized Calls to Action (CTAs) view for CSMs, which should ideally be automatically generated. The CTAs can be automatically created based on the customer journey phase and/or

CHAPTER 6   MAKING SENSE OF DATA

triggers related to customer health, risk assessment, etc. They can also be created manually by the CSMs based on their current customer account state and priorities. Reviewing the CTAs dashboard should be the starting point for a CSM's day at work. They'll be able to easily review the calls to action for a particular day or week and be able to take the appropriate action.

Table 6-4. *Prioritized CSM Calls to Action View*

Call to action	Customer name	ETA	CTA status	Dependency/ risk	Success plan	Current stage
Send customer onboarding plan	Cust 1	<date>	Green	None	<link to success plan> which has high level overall plan	Onboarding
Schedule business strategy meeting with customer exec sponsor	Cust 2	<date>		Customer exec sponsor on vacation and not available	<link to success plan>	Growth
....	...	....	...	....	....	....

We have now reviewed the key metrics and KPIs that are important to track for a Customer Success practice, how to match them to desired outcomes, and how to customize the dashboards for different roles.

Along with tracking data and metrics after the fact, it is also very important for a CS practice to appropriately manage revenue, growth, and heath forecasts. This is done via the forecasting models and dashboards. Forecasts-tracking dashboards are a key resource for CS leaders and managers for their long-term planning to appropriately budget and resource their teams.

Forecasting Dashboards

As a Customer Success leader and practitioner, it's very important for you to have a process to forecast your customers' retention, growth, and expansion metrics over the next quarter, year, or more. Without proper forecasting, you cannot plan for resources, budgets, and the evolution of your CS practice. CS forecasting is as much an art as it is a science. Some of the factors to consider for forecasting are the customer's lifetime value, current customer sentiment, customer use cases and expansion opportunities, consumption trends, and propensity insights.

Your CS forecasting models can be built into your CS tools or managed separately. Figure 6-15 shows an example of a CS forecasting tool and Figure 6-16 shows an example of a revenue tracking template. You and your CSMs should be able to fill models like these with your forecast values for appropriate adjustment, sign off, and tracking.

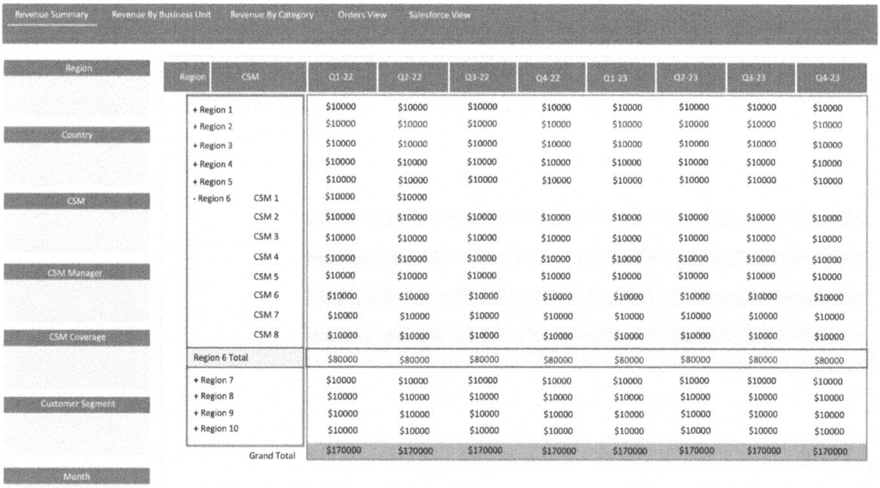

CHAPTER 6   MAKING SENSE OF DATA

Figure 6-15. *CS forecasting tool example*

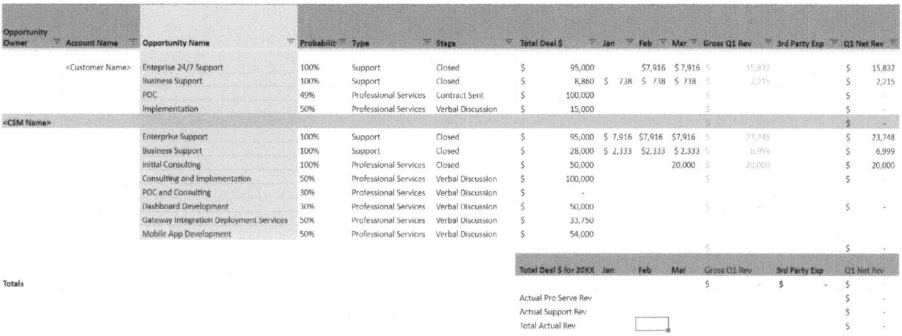

Figure 6-16. *CS revenue tracking template*

Now that we have a good understanding of the kinds of dashboards that can be built to set up a CS practice and CS Center of Excellence, let's take a look at how we can scale your CS practice by deploying scaling, optimization, and automation techniques.

CHAPTER 7

Designing Customer Success for Scale

A mid-size IT company was dealing with stagnating growth of revenues from its biggest customers. Many of those customers were not happy. They would have switched to a competitor at the first opportunity. The main things holding them back were the significant cost of switching to a competitor and certain differentiating product features that they liked.

That's why the company introduced a Customer Success practice to focus solely on increasing the engagement and improving the experience of these top customers to enhance growth and overall customer satisfaction. Once that goal was achieved, the company decided to expand the footprint of Customer Success to the rest of its customers, including enterprise and SMB. They wanted to do this in tandem with a broader transformation effort to move their business to a cloud-services model.

The challenge was, how much to invest to scale Customer Success, where to start, which areas to focus on, and how to do it properly. For example, the company had to decide, considering their investment capacity and the ROI, if they should invest in providing enterprise customers with access to the Customer Success team across their entire post-sales lifecycle or only in a specific phase like onboarding. Should they create a separate low-touch CSM team to service the enterprise and lower tier accounts? Or should they rely completely on an automated digital-touch experience for the lower tier customers?

CHAPTER 7 DESIGNING CUSTOMER SUCCESS FOR SCALE

These are the kinds of decisions many companies face as they introduce and expand their Customer Success practice. As they realize that focusing on customers' business outcomes and experience is an important driver for customer growth, there's an increased focus on how to expand Customer Success to all tiers of customers. Most companies, though, are restrained by budget and resources. They can offer proactive Customer Success engagement to only a small subset of their customers.

Some of the other factors that make scaling a Customer Success practice hard are external factors like talent shortage, or expectations from customers that they will get a high manual-touch experience at all times. There are internal factors too, like lack of budgets, skill sets, standard processes, and tools. Fear of change is also a big factor in stymieing many Customer Success scaling initiatives that require a change in the CS and company operational model.

In this chapter, we explore what is required to build a Customer Success practice designed for scale, and driven by a digital-touch approach.

At the core of this approach is timely access to data. Thanks to Internet of Things driven edge computing and SaaS driven listening posts, we already have access to near real-time data, which is used to drive product feature prioritizations, predict bugs, and make better products. But that data is also a gold mine that reveals how products and services are being used by customers, and how products are adopted.

It can be used to build and improve a company's customer-centric focus and growth models. Automations and triggers help predict churn risk, customer engagement, adoption, and satisfaction patterns based on product popularity, usage trends, and other parameters. Expanding and scaling your CS practice is therefore possible without blowing the budgets and resource requirements.

CHAPTER 7 DESIGNING CUSTOMER SUCCESS FOR SCALE

Figure 7-1 shows the evolution of customer engagement processes from a reactive to a proactive model. Standardization, repetitiveness, and operationalization of customer engagement workflows are critical for evolving from a reactive to a proactive, predictive, and repeatable CS operational model. Activities like risk and churn management, value analysis and articulation, and timely customer communications are automated and executed at scale across all customer tiers, and internally within the company, as well. As discussed in previous chapters, these activities are driven by CS Ops teams like the Customer Success Center of Excellence (CS CoE) that are focused on standardizing and operationalizing CS.

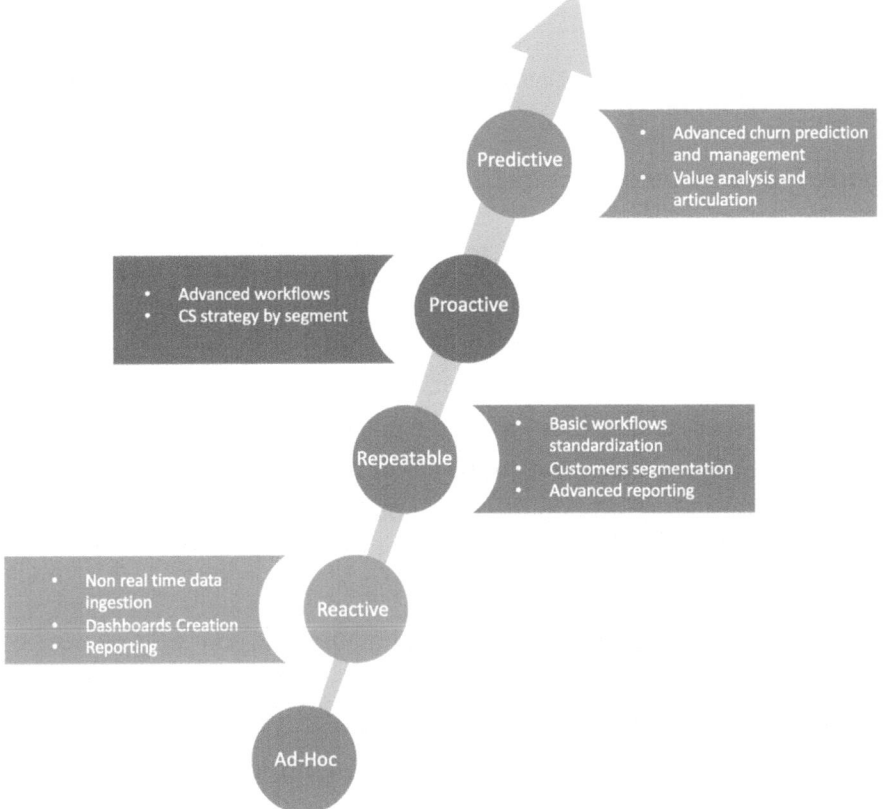

Figure 7-1. *Customer Success evolution from reactive to proactive*

CHAPTER 7 DESIGNING CUSTOMER SUCCESS FOR SCALE

How to Build Customer Success for Scale

There are multiple ways to scale a Customer Success practice. But irrespective of your approach, consider the framework shown in Figure 7-2 to ask the relevant questions and understand the key decision points to keep in mind when building and scaling your CS practice. The PPT (People, Process, Technology) framework has been around since the 1960s and is still very relevant today for improving the operational efficiencies of your team and tools. We have added an additional component to it; Data.

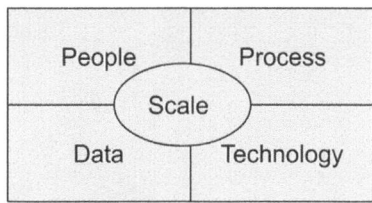

Figure 7-2. Customer Success scaling framework

People

What experience and skill sets do your Customer Success resources have? Do they understand the philosophies and methodologies of Customer Success? Do they have experience working with different Customer Success engagement models (high touch, low touch, fully automated, etc.) and be able to support them? Consider bringing your entire Customer Success team to a common baseline by having them go through Customer Success certifications.

Processes

What is the functional and operational maturity of your CS practice? How well are the workflows and playbooks defined? What kind of CS engagement model are they mapped to currently? What would it take to extend them beyond the current models and/or introduce digital touch?

Data and Technology

What kind of data, telemetry, and tools do you have access to that you can leverage to scale your CS practice? What are the gaps? Do you have a standard CS data model across your company?

Once you answer the preceding questions, you can decide which methodology you want to use to scale your CS practice, and you can do it a few different ways. You can grow your Customer Success team linearly as your customer accounts grow to service those accounts. You can do this cost effectively by leveraging partners to manage your growing customer base or by setting up cost-efficient, offshore customer success hubs to manage your mid- and lower-tier accounts. These are popular models that are currently used by many companies. Alternatively, or in tandem with manual scaling approaches, you can leverage technology (digital touch), gradually increasing the footprint of the digital-led engagement model and reducing reliance on manual-driven engagement models. We will look at this approach in more detail in this chapter.

Digital-Driven Customer Success Model

Digital-driven Customer Success is an increasingly popular scaling model since it helps companies scale their CS practices without the requirement of linearly adding CSMs to manually manage the growing number of accounts. Initial investment and commitment is needed to develop and deploy a digital-driven customer success model. However, once it is deployed properly, it should be easily expandable with minimal investment as your customer base grows.

As shown in Figure 7-3, you begin laying the foundation stones for a digital-driven engagement model by defining and standardizing your data models, tools, and assets. Then you can start digital-driven engagement for a subsection of customers and continue to gradually increase the digital customer-engagement footprint across all tiers. Leveraging a digital-touch engagement model driven by self-serve and automation methodologies is

CHAPTER 7 DESIGNING CUSTOMER SUCCESS FOR SCALE

NOT only for your long-tail customers. If you design it right, it can become a key differentiator for your Customer Success practice and enhance your CX model for all customer tiers.

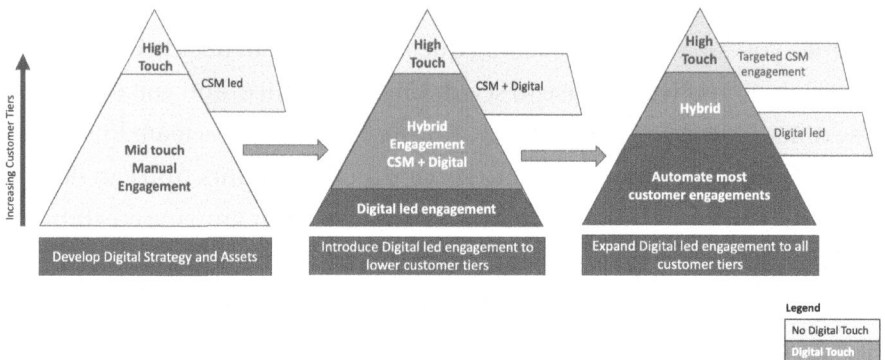

Figure 7-3. Digital-driven Customer Success evolution model

Anuj Nadkarni, a senior CS executive who has driven CS digital transformations in Fortune 500 companies, elaborates on the guiding principles of Digital CS (as shown in Figure 7-4) as follows:

> Digital-driven customer engagement can be a game changer for companies looking to both scale their Customer Success practices and enhance their customer experience without breaking their budgets. It is important to remember the following guiding principles when building your digital engagement model. Be sure to plug in the digital engagement touchpoints throughout the customer journey and not just in specific phases. Make sure to leverage all available digital channels in your engagement model to ensure an optimal experience. Lead with a digital-first engagement mindset, i.e., when operationalizing your CS journey maps, processes and standards, start by identifying what steps you can digitize and then add the manual intervention steps instead of leading with a manual-first approach. Last but certainly not least, make sure that your digital engagements are targeted

and personalized to your customers. That will be key to ensuring a good customer experience and to separate your digital-driven engagement model from marketing-type campaigns and communications.

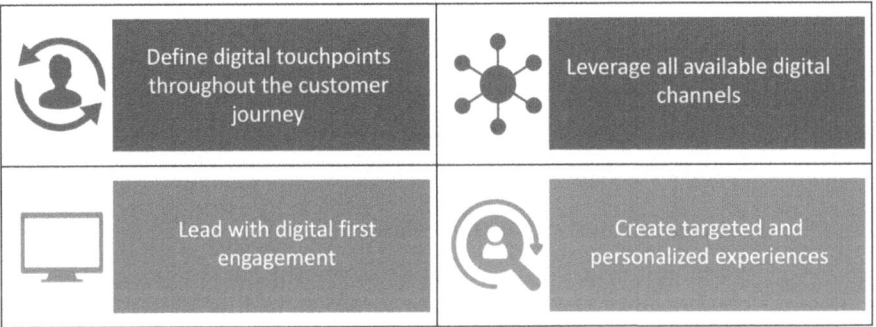

Figure 7-4. Guiding principles of digital-driven Customer Success

To scale a Customer Success and Engagement model and convert it into a digitized and automated, or semi-automated, proactive methodology, the following foundational elements are required:

- A master customer data model that identifies a unique customer across all the different tools and systems in a company

- A unified customer 360 view built by pulling data from different systems

- Defined customer journey maps and playbooks that are your starting point for building your scaling model

- Proper change management to ensure adoption and propagation of the new standardized data and engagement models in a consistent manner across your organization

CHAPTER 7   DESIGNING CUSTOMER SUCCESS FOR SCALE

There are some foundational steps that you have to put in place to scale a customer success practice to comply with the preceding requirements. They are as follows:

1. **Data modeling for standardization**

    a. Build a customer data model that can be standardized across your enterprise to capture and propagate customer data across multiple workflows and tools.

    b. Build unified customer dashboards with relevant info captured for different functions. For example, a dashboard with top product features that is monitored by the product team, a dashboard of top tickets for the Support team, a customer journey dashboard for the CS team, an executive customer dashboard that highlights the ARR growth and trends, and so on. A unified customer 360 system should consolidate all the customer data in a single view.

2. **Picking the right tools and processes**

    a. Build your overall customer journey map with the relevant playbooks for phases like onboarding, adoption, expansion, and renew/refresh. You could be using this journey map for your high-touch customers, but you should be able to adopt the same model with some changes and simplifications for your digital touch Customer Success as well. Building all your journey maps and playbooks by identifying and planning for potential digital touchpoints

CHAPTER 7   DESIGNING CUSTOMER SUCCESS FOR SCALE

   upfront will make it easier to adapt and scale your playbooks to a digital-driven or digital-incorporated engagement model when you are ready for it.

   b. Identify workflows that can be fully automated vs. partially automated, their prioritization, and the target audience. For example, you could choose to begin expanding your CS footprint by automating your onboarding touch points or your customer health monitoring triggers for your mid- or lower-tier customers. If these customers currently have no access to the Customer Success team, providing a standardized, automated digital touch experience could be a big step forward from their current onboarding experience.

   c. Also, do your due diligence to identify the right Customer Success tool that will be the backbone of your Customer Success practice, where you will deploy all your playbooks, best practices, and digital-driven automations.

3. **Getting buy-in**

   a. Getting buy-in from your Sales, Services, Support, Product and Executive Leadership team is an often-overlooked but extremely important step in making a Customer Success digital touch and scaling initiative successful. These functions have to be aligned on the customer data model and workflows standardization initiatives since it could

155

impact the way they do things currently. It is also extremely important to get buy-in from the executive leadership team since the scaling processes being introduced could fundamentally change the way customer data is being tracked and used in your company.

b. You will need to invest in CS Ops resources, tools, and training. Make sure you have the budget approved for these initiatives and the required headcounts.

4. **Executing incrementally**

a. Run a pilot with a limited set of customers to introduce the Customer Success digital touch model. You could choose to implement this model just for your long-tail customers in the introductory phase. Or you could run a pilot to collect feedback across multiple customer tiers. It is your choice, depending on what your desired outcomes are from the pilot. If you choose to engage customers from different tiers in the pilot, you might want to execute a different operational model for each of the tiers. For example, you could deploy a fully self-serve digital touch execution model for your enterprise and lower-tier customers and a semi-automated model for your strategic customers. That way, you can continue to give them the white glove treatment with a human touch, which is enhanced with the self-serve processes you have put in place. And/or you could pick

CHAPTER 7 DESIGNING CUSTOMER SUCCESS FOR SCALE

a single phase of the customer journey to do your pilot. For example, start by automating the customer onboarding process for your long-tail customers by introducing automated onboarding communications and tracking, like welcome letters, onboarding steps triggers and emails, etc.

b. Capture in great detail the feedback from pilot customers (both internal and external) on what's working well and the gaps. Iterate, redeploy, and gradually expand.

c. Be prepared for some customers to be more receptive and even appreciate a digital touch approach vs. others, irrespective of their tier. Try to include a good sampling of your customer profiles in your pilot to identify any themes or patterns of behavior. For example, do your SaaS customers prefer a more hands-off CS approach compared to your manufacturing customers, who might like a more human-led, hands-on approach?

d. Be prepared to take it slow in the first few iterations of deployment and do not get disheartened even if you receive negative feedback or low adoption initially, especially from customers who are used to a very high touch, manually intensive type of engagement. Be confident that strategically planning and building for scale is the right thing to do, both for your company and to make sure that you are able to give the best possible engagement experience for all your customers.

e. Handling change management with internal and external stakeholders is the key difference between success and failure. Make sure you address any concerns that your internal team members and/or cross-functional stakeholders might have about the impact of introducing a digital-driven approach on their current customer engagement models and/or any perceived threats to their jobs because of the introduction of automations. Also make sure you address any concerns that your customers might have about the loss of direct engagement because of the introduction of this new engagement model. It is very important that all your stakeholders view this change in a positive light and clearly understand what's in it for them.

Let us now delve deeper into the areas of data modeling and tooling for designing and building a Customer Success practice for scale.

CS Data Modeling for Standardization
Customer Data Model

In this section, we'll explore how to create a unified customer data model across multiple internal systems that store customer data. The ultimate goal is to build a common customer 360 dashboard.

CHAPTER 7   DESIGNING CUSTOMER SUCCESS FOR SCALE

A unified and easy-to-use customer data model will help identify each of your customers uniquely (via unique identifiers), create a common nomenclature of standard naming conventions for fields to capture customer-related information (field labels, variable names, etc.) and be pluggable, referenceable, and reusable across multiple tools. It will help you encode, map, and track customer account information in commonly used tools like Salesforce, Jira, and others.

Once you have encoded your customer data model, you can create customer 360 dashboards that will act as your CS central nervous system. As discussed in the previous chapter, the customer 360 dashboard can help track customer health, growth indicators, support issues, product blockers, feature requests, feedback, etc. It can also enable the cross-functional teams to track required customer info in a consistent way to prioritize areas under their control by assessing impact. The information flow to and from your central Customer Success tool and/or customer 360 tool and other internal systems can be bi-directional. Appropriate rules and triggers should be defined to make sure that data integrity and accuracy is maintained at all times.

The following are some of the desired outcomes from the data modeling exercise:

- **Data Integrity across different tools:** Standard data model and easy management of customer data across different tools.

- **Issues and Activity tracking:** A single set of dashboards that will be the source of truth for Engineering, Product, CS, Sales, and Support with regards to account-specific tasks/issues that are currently logged in different tools, which have highest priority and impact and who are the primary responsible stakeholders.

- **Trigger Setting:** Ability to set triggers and fire rules based on certain conditions. The triggers should be tied to notifications and/or actions.

- **Report Generation:** Ability to download, filter, and review reports from these dashboards for specific time periods or defined criteria.

- **Automation of commonly used workflows:** Ability to propagate scaling and self-serve engagement models.

After understanding the importance of building a unified customer data model and the desired outcomes, the next step is to create an action plan for building and standardizing it across relevant internal systems. An action plan will help you identify the high-level steps that are needed, such as the internal systems you need to integrate with and the corresponding cross-functional teams who need to sign off on building your unified data model and customer 360 system.

Action Plan for Building a Standardized Customer Data Model

As you build your customer data model, you should start thinking in parallel about the tool in which you will be deploying your data model and the customer 360 nerve center it will drive. Your customer 360 system will maintain a unified view of your consolidated customer data. Once you have the right tool for deploying your customer 360 dashboards, your action plan should factor in how to move data from internal systems to and from this tool to ensure data integrity and consistency.

Trust us, this exercise sounds more difficult than it actually is. Think about it. Even today, you use a myriad of tools to track your customers' health and adoption, including support/ticket-tracking tools, ops/adoption-tracking tools, sales-tracking tools, and delivery-tracking tools.

All we are doing here is consolidating all that customer info into a single unified system, and you could build, buy, or leverage an existing tool for the task. From this, different views for different audiences (executive team, account team, product team, customer, etc.) can be easily created and, ideally, automated. Most of the information you need is likely being captured in some form or other already. What now needs to be done is to bring all that information together. That way, you can get an accurate picture of a customer's current health and opportunities for growth, plus the ability to forecast future retention, health, and expansion.

Let's look at a sample action plan to build a customer data model leading up to building a customer 360 system, as shown in Table 7-1.

Let's look at a sample customer data model built by following Step 1 of the action plan shown in Table 7-1.

Table 7-1. *Action Plan to Create a Customer 360 Dashboard*

Step	Description
Step 1	Create the customer data model and nomenclature with a goal of mapping all the Customer Accounts info across different tools in a standard way.
Step 2	Review existing fields in existing tools and map/edit the fields to align to the defined customer data model.
Step 3	Add new or updated fields to your customer 360 system and other tools as needed to track customer health, prioritizations, and responsibilities. Remove irrelevant fields.
Step 4	Share the new Customer data model model with all relevant internal stakeholders; what the fields mean, which ones are required vs. optional, and so on.
Step 5	Create a unified customer 360 dashboard(s) for the entire company.

Sample Customer Data Model

Table 7-2 shows a sample customer data model. The goal of defining this model is to define fields and a standard nomenclature to uniquely identify and map a customer account across all of the company's internal tools that stores customer information. This enables easy tracking of customer information across different tools and building of a unified customer 360 system to monitor customer health and activity.

Table 7-2. Sample Customer Data Model

Field name	Description	Examples
Customer ID	Unique Identifier for the customer account across all systems, products, and tools of a company. Should be created in one primary CRM tool and then mapped to all other tools to log the customer info	<Cust123> or < RegionID.Cust123>: if your customers are local to regions and not global
Customer Name	Unique customer name that is mapped to Customer ID and stays the same in all internal tools. Should be input in primary CRM tool only at the time of the customer record creation	Example: "Apple Inc" or "Intel Inc," etc. and mapped in the overall hierarchy as <Customer ID>.<Customer Name>
RegionID	Unique ID for a particular region your company operates in	Example: RegionNA; RegionEMEA; etc.
Business unit ID	Unique ID for customer business units your company works with	Example: BUFinance, BUProduct, etc.

(*continued*)

Table 7-2. (*continued*)

Field name	Description	Examples
Customer entity ID	Child to Customer ID. Created through a combination of Customer ID and customer region and/or Customer BU, etc. to identify the key customer entity with whom you are engaging For example, you could be working with the customer's product team in EMEA region. You could also be separately working with the customer's product team in APAC region. To track the work you do with both teams appropriately, you can map the right Customer Entity ID to your contracts or Salesforce opportunities	Cust123.RegionNA. BUProduct
End Customer ID (optional - where applicable)	Child to Customer ID. Unique ID to track the end customers of your own customers • Could be applicable in partner/reseller or OEM scenario where customers might be selling your product as part of their own offering and you need to track their end customers. • You can create your customer's or partner's end customer IDs and names within your CRM or they will be provided to you by your partner or customer	<CustomerID. endCustomerID> <CustABC.EndCust1> <CustABC.EndCust2>

(*continued*)

Table 7-2. (*continued*)

Field name	Description	Examples
End Customer Name optional - where applicable)	Unique name mapped to End Customer ID to track the end customers of your own customers (applicable in partner/ reseller or OEM scenario where customer might be selling your product as part of their own offering and you need to track their end customers)	<CustomerID. endCustomerID. endCustomerName>
And so on		

Once you have identified all the fields for your customer data model, revisit the customer info logged in your existing Support, Product, and other tools and add or update fields in those systems as needed to align with the defined customer data model. For example, these tools might not have the same field names for customer IDs or customer names as defined in your master data model. Or they might have defined customer ID values that are local to their own systems and hence would have to be updated and mapped based on values in the central customer data model. Or some of the key fields to assess customer health might be missing.

Once customer ID, name, etc. are defined in a customer master record, all references to those fields in other systems should only be made via selection from a preexisting menu (like drop-downs) instead of allowing free text entry. This is best practice to avoid typing errors or misspellings that could break the mapping of the data from these systems back to the customer master record.

Also, some of the internal tools might require the addition of new fields that are needed to track feature/issue prioritizations and responsibilities, etc. At a minimum, it is helpful for all internal systems to log the below customer info so that all internal teams have the pulse of the customer at all times:

CHAPTER 7   DESIGNING CUSTOMER SUCCESS FOR SCALE

- Customer/Account Name: selected from a prepopulated list that is pulled from the centralized CS system

- End Customer Name (optional): If customer is a Partner/Reseller and has end customers

- Type/Stage of business (New > onboarding, Existing > growth, upsell, customer/user experience, performance, etc.) (drop-down pick-list)

- Customer Success Manager – automatically populated based on Customer/Account Name/ID

- Sales rep – automatically populated based on Customer/Account Name/ID

- Business upside (if there is a compelling business situation that stakeholders need to be aware of, like an upcoming renewal or upsell opportunity) – only required if Business Type is Onboarding or Growth or Upsell

- Month/Year of upside: to assess the urgency

Logging the preceding information about customers in internal systems provides teams like Support, Product, Engineering, and others context on where the customer is and how they should be prioritizing customer-related requests, keeping in context any compelling upcoming business events like renewal and/or expansion deals.

As part of this exercise, identify any fields that need to be removed that are not being used or are redundant. Once you determine the right data model for your CS practice and have defined your customer journey maps and playbooks, the next step is to determine the right toolsets to deploy them in.

CHAPTER 7   DESIGNING CUSTOMER SUCCESS FOR SCALE

Picking the Right Tools

Figure 7-5. *Customer Success tools*

As shown in Figure 7-5, customer engagement activities are typically not managed by a single tool. Once you have your standard data model ready, it is extremely important to zero in on the workflows, processes, and tools that are required to log and track your customer info across different tools and systems, either manually or with some level of automation for scaling.

CHAPTER 7   DESIGNING CUSTOMER SUCCESS FOR SCALE

Depending on your specific requirements, you can pick the tools that best serve your needs. There are a myriad of customer engagement tools available, as shown in Table 7-3.

Table 7-3. *Customer Engagement tools*

Type of tool	Use	Examples
Customer Success management tools	Tools that help map customer journeys and major post-sales engagement milestones, health scoring, calls to action, etc. These tools can become the primary day-to-day working tool for your Customer Success Managers.	Strikedeck, Gainsight, ChurnZero, Totango, Catalyst, Vitally etc
Customer onboarding tools	Manage customer onboarding projects for customers of different sizes.	Rocketlane, OnRamp, OnBoard etc.
Customer 360 tools	Tools that capture data from different systems to offer a consolidated customer view. Your CS Management tools can offer a C360 capability, or in some cases your C360 tool can be stand-alone and incorporated into your overall CS tool as a plug-in.	Could be same as your Customer Success Management tools or separately built in-house for a broader audience if the CS tools are limited to CS team usage only.
Survey tools	Customers that help conduct CSAT, NPS surveys.	SurveyMonkey, TechValidate, Qualtrics, etc.

(*continued*)

Table 7-3. (*continued*)

Type of tool	Use	Examples
Support tools	Your Support team might already be using some tools, so it's important to know about them and have the ability to pull data from those tools to your C360 tool/workflows.	Supportal, Zendesk, etc.
CRM tools	Tools that help manage customer account data and activity.	Salesforce, HubSpot, Zoho, Affinity etc
Content management tools	Tools that help manage and disseminate content and communications to customers (marketing tools, LMS tools, websites, etc.)	

Do your due diligence to pick the right tools to best serve your customer engagement and scaling needs. Do not be intimidated by the variety of tools out there. If you have your customer data model, data integration, and display requirements and engagement workflows defined, picking the tools should be a relatively simple exercise. Some consideration criteria, that you could use as a checklist, are

- What kind of a tool are you looking for – A CS management tool, a customer 360 tool, a CRM tool or a combination?

- What are some of the non-negotiable activities that the tool needs to be able to do? For you, it may be extremely important that it comes with predefined customer journey flows or that it's able to send automated notifications to customers by integrating with email systems, or that it allows for the creation of manual or automated rules and/or action triggers for certain events, etc.

- Can the tool integrate with your current tech stack being used by Product, Support, Eng, etc. to pull or push data from/to those systems as needed?

- What is the ramp-up time/effort and first time to value timeline (approx.) and would that work for you?

- Is the tool easy and intuitive to use? Will your CS team adapt quickly to using it?

- What does the off-ramp time/process look like if you decide that things are not working out?

- How is your customer and company data managed within the tool? Do the privacy and security protocols align with your company's requirements?

- Build vs. Buy: Does it make sense for you to invest in purchasing a CS tool or does it make more sense to build one in-house, considering your setup?

Remember that your tech stack is the execution backbone of your operational model. If the tools do not execute and deliver properly and cannot support your defined processes effectively then you will not be able to derive 100% ROI and value from your CS Org and setup. This is the case no matter how good your journey maps, processes, scaling methodologies, and data models might be.

Once you have your customer journey maps and playbooks defined and your tech stack identified and deployed with the right processes, you can look at optimization, scaling, and customer engagement enhancement opportunities by leveraging automations.

Digital-Driven Process Automations

Digital Touch (also known as Tech Touch) is the latest buzzword in Customer Success. And with good reason. Customer Success is about providing the best possible experience to your customers to promote the attainment of their desired outcomes. It builds their loyalty and forms a partnership that positively influences your company's growth and ARR. You might assume that providing this level of service would require intensive and hands-on interaction, but this is not the case. In this day and age, standardization and scale can be achieved using automations driven by tools and data-driven triggers and actions. Indeed, the industry of Customer Success tools came to being as a result of the philosophy that Customer Success methodology can be standardized and automated to a certain extent.

Digital-driven automations are the medium by which you can expand your Customer Success practice to all your customers; not just your most important ones. So it is important to consider opportunities to automate and plan for them as you build your Customer Success practice, journey maps, and playbooks.

Which Processes Are Candidates for Automating?

The first step in identifying target processes for automations is to define your customer's journey. Once the journey or journeys are defined, the next step is to identify which of the journey components have standard playbooks. For example, are there standard steps to be followed for all customer onboardings or onboardings for a segment of customers? Are there customer health scores or leading risk indicators that can be automatically monitored with triggerable actions? Do these steps have a detailed playbook? Can they be tracked using tools so that manual interventions can be plugged into the process as needed?

CHAPTER 7   DESIGNING CUSTOMER SUCCESS FOR SCALE

Figure 7-6 shows a sample digital customer journey with examples of digital triggers and actions and delivery mediums.

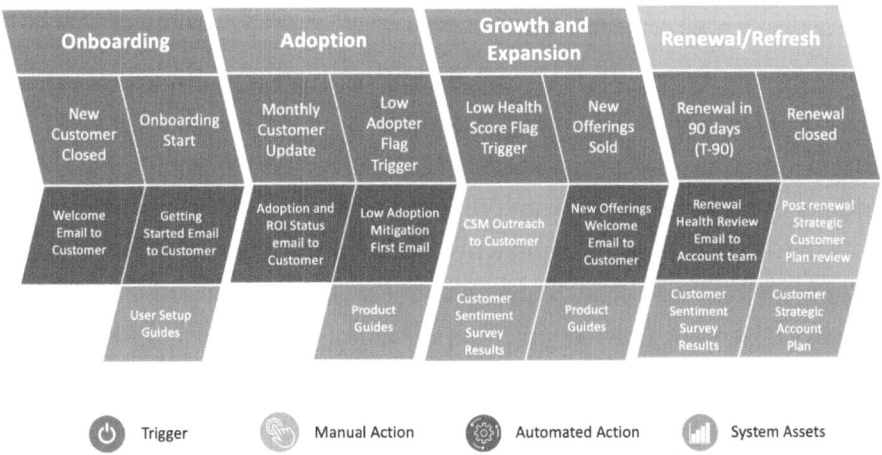

Figure 7-6. Sample digital-led customer journey with triggers and actions

Not all steps in a workflow can or may need to be fully automated. The goal should be to have a level of standardization and automation for all baseline repeatable and trackable processes. For example, the following could be some of the considerations when automating a customer onboarding process:

- Can you automate/templatize the first customer contact email after the account is handed to CS?

- Can the system automatically notify the customer about upcoming onboarding actions and milestones?

- Can the system send you reminders in case of customer inaction?

- Can the system track customer onboarding health and escalate, if needed?

171

Similarly, monthly or quarterly customer updates could be good candidates for automations. This will likely require some collaboration with other teams like Product, Support, Marketing, etc. Together, you identify what information to share with customers, such as new product updates, analysts' reports and market trends. You can combine that with customized info, like a customer's adoption stats, tickets analysis, their desired outcomes and progression, etc. These types of automations will require consolidation of information from multiple systems, but it should be doable once templatized and will reduce significant manual work for not only Customer Success Managers but also for other customer-facing personnel like your Services and Support team members.

Manjula Talreja, Chief Customer Officer of PagerDuty, explains how they are revolutionizing the digital-led support escalations management by introducing Intelligent Swarming:

> "Intelligent Swarming is the framework by which a Support case owner (often a customer service agent) shares customer case information with a team of cross functional experts to work together on resolution. Customer service agents leverage real-time service data, historical incidence context and monitoring data from technical systems across the organization to share a holistic view of the issue. Agents also utilize predefined action triggers to automate mundane workflows associated with escalations management like setting up a conference bridge, subscribing additional stakeholders to the incident, and publishing status updates. These actions can be automatically triggered based on specific incident types or manually initiated as needed. Some automated processes, depending on the type of workflow, might still need manual oversight, especially in situations where a human action is needed to complete the process or to deal with escalations. Having human oversight on all automated processes is key to ensure that the processes are working as expected.

But this is where the power of PagerDuty's automation and machine learning translates to true value for our customers. We use this type of automation to drive better uptime for a company, better coordination between their staff, and ultimately, a better experience for *their* customers.

I often say a consumer doesn't remember a disruption from a brand they love – but they will remember the *experience*. Empowering PagerDuty customers to be proactive and informed in the moments when their brand reputation is on the line is where we create the most value, and a critical moment in what we call our customer lifecycle. We use that term intentionally. A customer's experience with PagerDuty isn't linear, with a beginning and an end – we move from purchase, to implementation and adoption, to value generation, to the renewal or adoption of additional products to facilitate digital operations maturity, and the cycle starts again. When we're doing our job as a CS team, we are demonstrating value to customers every step of the way, anticipating their future needs, understanding their business imperatives, and acting as a trusted partner to apply our technology to advance their strategy." =.

Once you have finalized your customer journey, identified key workflows like onboarding, adoption, expansion, status reporting, escalations, deployment management, etc., and created the step-by-step playbooks and related artifacts as described in previous chapters and have identified the necessary tools and dashboards, you are now ready to automate.

How to Automate?

Let us now look at the key components that need to be considered when you are looking to automate your processes and workflows? They include date-based triggers and milestones definitions, as shown in Table 7-4.

Table 7-4. The Five Key Components for Automating a Workflow

Method	Description	Examples
Date-based triggers for entry and exit	Rules to indicate when an automated process or action needs to be triggered and when it's completed	Start trigger(s): • Updating Customer Account Status to "Closed-Won" in Salesforce AND Customer Journey Status changed to "Onboarding" could trigger the automated onboarding workflows End trigger: • Customer Journey Status changed to "Adoption" or whatever is the next phase after onboarding is complete
Related content and assets	The key assets that need to be sent or received as part of the automated process	• Standard customer-facing onboarding checklist or deck to the customer • Receiving an onboarding form from the customer outlining their requirements, etc.
Milestones definitions	What are the key milestones that are part of the automated processes?	• Onboarding call • Post-onboarding call follow-up • Success plan creation • Success plan sign-off

(*continued*)

CHAPTER 7 DESIGNING CUSTOMER SUCCESS FOR SCALE

Table 7-4. (*continued*)

Method	Description	Examples
Data analytics	Tracking the key milestones, deliverables, and triggers via dashboards for monitoring and triggering the right remediation actions at the right time	• Customer's onboarding dashboard • Call to actions dashboard • Risks dashboard
Remediation actions	Actions that are needed to keep the workflow healthy and progressing	• Manual intervention to nudge customer to finish onboarding steps • Automated reminder email to customer to start onboarding process

A standard automation process would consist of the following steps as shown in Figure 7-7.

CHAPTER 7   DESIGNING CUSTOMER SUCCESS FOR SCALE

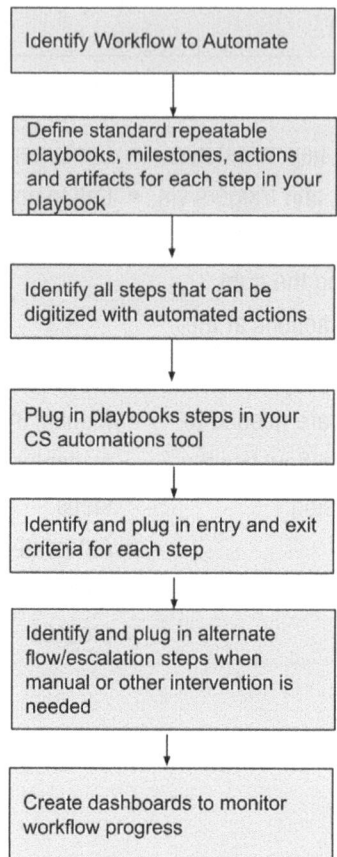

Figure 7-7. Customer workflow process automations steps

The actual automation process can be simple or complex based on the complexity of the workflow being automated. Let us now look at a few automation examples.

Automation Examples

Example1: New Customer Contact Welcome Note Automation Example

Automation Start Trigger points examples:

- When the Salesforce opportunity status changes to "closed won"
- When a new customer contact is added to an existing customer account and identified as a system user

Automation complexity: Easy to Medium
Delivery Mechanism: Email
Email recipients: Customer contacts in Salesforce Opportunity or onboarding contact identified in Customer Success tool

Template
Hi <customer name>

We would like to thank you for choosing <your company name>. In the following, you will find useful information that we invite you to share with your team. In case of any questions or clarifications, please do not hesitate to reach out to the Customer Success team.

Your Subscription Information:

Qty	Product	Description	Type	Level	Licensed devices	Subscription term

Technical Support

The preceding subscriptions to our Enterprise License include access to our Technical Support team. Please follow the following steps to set up your Support account. Click the icons to find out more:

Helpful Resources to Get Started

Again, thank you very much for your business, do not hesitate to let us know if there is anything we can do to further help you get started.

Regards,

Customer Success Team

Example 2: Complex Onboarding Workflow Automation

Onboarding is the process of helping a new customer to perform the setup, integrations, and/or installations required for them to start receiving the benefit(s) of using your products and services. Onboarding can also include knowledge transfer and/or training to provide your customer with the essential skillset to work with the newly purchased technology.

In many cases, the exact process for onboarding is unique to your company and the actions your company performs is predicated on key dates or milestones described in the customer journey. Incorporate

Date-Based Action Triggers to decrease your time to value and help your customers to start using your products and services quickly and smoothly.

Automation start trigger points examples:

- Triggered when customer is ready to start onboarding (trigger point could vary based on the company)

- When CRM opportunity is closed and won and a new contact is added to the opportunity

Automation complexity: Varies based on your product

Delivery Mechanism: Series of Emails or online forms + support and enablement self-serve tools + internal CS tools to track progress and initiate next steps till end of phase

Customer participants: Customer participants in this process should be identified either by the Sales team or by the CS team in the pre-onboarding phase before onboarding officially starts.

Figure 7-8 shows an example of an onboarding automation workflow for an online advertising campaign management Platform as a Service company (PaaS). The Customer Success Managers help manage the customers' monthly advertising campaign budgets through the platform to make sure that customers are attaining their desired business outcomes by posting their online ads. on different sites like Google, Facebook, and other targeted publisher websites through the company's platform. The platform ingests the customers ads. daily via an XML feed. There could also be different customer types. Some customers directly post their own ads. using the platform. Others are agencies who are posting ads. on behalf of their end customers and need end customers-level budgets and outcomes tracking and reporting.

Onboarding in this example involves multiple steps like creating the new master customer record and instance on the platform and in the CS tool (if one does not exist), setting up the customer's XML data feed to the platform, validating the feed to make sure that it is following the right schema for auto ingestion, setting up engagement flows depending on whether the customer is on a managed services or a self-serve engagement model. Many of the setup, monitoring, and engagement steps can be automated to expedite onboarding, reduce human intervention, and minimize human setup errors.

This is an advanced workflow that not only identifies the onboarding steps but also identifies the decision points and event triggers. You can create similar workflow models and flowcharts to clearly sketch out your onboarding steps and dependencies to identify which of those steps can be digitized and automated.

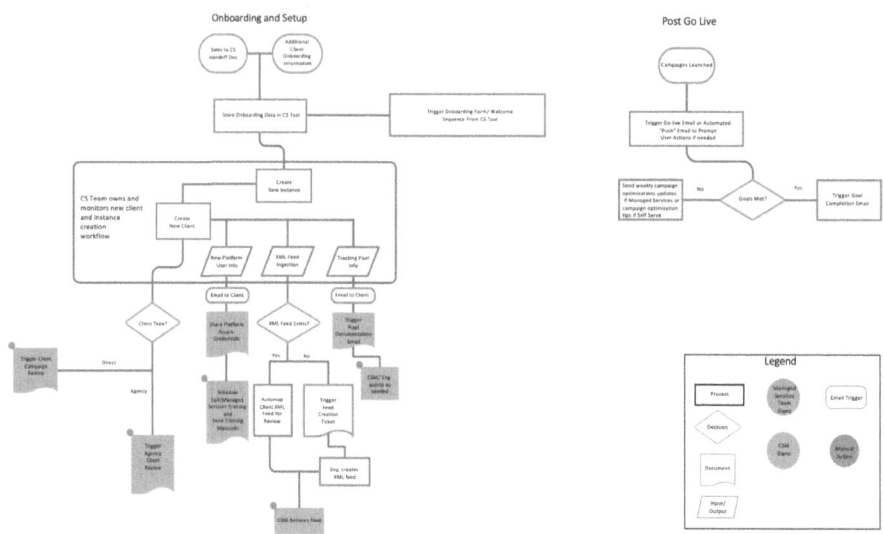

Figure 7-8. Example of complex onboarding automation flow

In this chapter, we elaborated on the value of a digital-led CS engagement model for scaling a CS practice and reviewed the best practices and foundational components to create such a model. We reviewed examples of how to create a unified customer data model and how to incorporate that model to build a customer 360 system. We discussed how you can identify the best candidate processes for automating and described a template for building out automations. We ended by reviewing a couple of process automation examples, one easy and another complex. In the next chapter, we will review the org. setup and roles to create a CS operations function like the CS CoE and how they help scale your CS practice.

CHAPTER 8

Role of CS Operations in Scaling a CS Practice

Customer Success Operations team provides standardization, intelligence, planning, and ultimately, strategy for your Customer Success practice.

To examine one way of building out your CS Ops team, let us return to our fictional SaaS company, SoftCorp. When Janice, their Chief Customer Officer, came on board and started the CS practice, SoftCorp's Customer Success footprint was limited to only their top strategic customers.

Janice understood the importance of extending that footprint to SoftCorp's remaining customers to maximize their ARR and customer experience. However, she did not have the building blocks to do so in a cost-effective manner. Janice initially turned to her company's Sales Ops team for help with activities like operationalizing customer journey maps and capturing and analyzing key data points and trends regarding customer health for forecasting and engagement planning purposes. SoftCorp's Sales Ops. team created some dashboards to capture CS metrics and tried to provide the necessary coverage for CS operational and analytical needs. But their primary focus was to support the needs of the Sales team. CS needs took a backseat because of bandwidth, resourcing, or other competing priorities.

© Chitra Madhwacharyula, Shreesha Ramdas 2023
C. Madhwacharyula and S. Ramdas, *Scaling Customer Success*,
https://doi.org/10.1007/978-1-4842-9192-4_8

So Janice hired a handful of CS operatives within her team to focus exclusively on CS operations. As the CS practice grew, Janice evolved her CS Ops. subfunction to a full-fledged CS Center of Excellence (CoE) and hired a worldwide Head of CS CoE to manage the function, whose scope of responsibilities included CS workflows definitions and standardization, tools management, learning and enablement, community and partners management. The CS Ops-focused CoE became an indispensable contributor to the success of Janice's CS practice. The CS CoE rolled up to Janice's CS Org. initially but, as the company grew, it eventually moved away from Janice's direct leadership to become part of a centralized Global Operations function, rolling up to the COO.

In this chapter, we will specifically look at the value and ways of setting up a CS operations function; whether it is a formal operations-focused Customer Success CoE or a smaller ops subfunction; and its benefits to scale and optimize a Customer Success practice.

Let's start by answering some common questions about Customer Success Operations, beginning with the most basic question of all.

What Is a Customer Success Operations Function?

A Customer Success operations-focused function, like a CS CoE, is a sub-function within CS or within your company's generic Operations team, with a focus on setting up and managing the operations of all things Customer Success.

The goal of a CS Operations Center of Excellence (CS CoE) is to standardize, optimize, simplify, and scale CS operations for maximum efficiency, effectiveness, and transparency. This could also include supporting operations for areas like professional and consulting services, customer account management, customer onboarding, support, education, training, and partner operations.

The scope of responsibilities of CS Ops. includes activities like identifying the right way to operationalize customer engagement workflows and playbooks for scale and efficiency, and making sure that the right metrics are being captured in the right frequency. It also involves setting up dashboards to display captured metrics to different audiences, advising on and tracking customer retention and growth forecasting, and driving strategic projects for the customer success organization. A key goal is to provide accurate and timely information flow to CS and company leadership and to CS team members to enable optimal and actionable decision-making.

Similar to the preceding SoftCorp example, many companies start with hiring a few CS Ops personnel to begin with; which makes perfect sense. Rather than set up a formal CS CoE on day one of building your CS practice, it's better to first build up your overall Customer Success organizational strategy, with primary focus on hiring your CSMs and mapping them to customer accounts.

Once your CS practice for your top-tier customers is fully set up (which is where most companies start their CS function), then the question arises: How do you scale CS to the next tier or all tiers of customers? And that's when you might want to start thinking about building out a full-fledged Customer Success Center of Excellence with focus on scaling your CS operations across different customer tiers, regions, business units, and solution offerings.

What Is the Value of a CS Operations/CS CoE Function to a CS Org?

Similar to how Sales organizations rely on their Sales Operations functions, having a CS Operations function becomes very important as CS Orgs. grow and become bigger. It would drive and manage the activities like the following:

- Track and measure CS tasks and milestones.
- Establish a data-driven approach to the CS practice.
    - Ensure that the right metrics and KPIs are being captured.
    - Ensure that the captured metrics and KPIs are being analyzed correctly.
    - Ensure that key findings are being translated into outcomes-based actions.
- Plan and optimize mapping and resourcing of CS resources effectively, based on CS pipeline and forecasting models.
- Define and automate key CS workflows by using the right tools and set up the right automation processes.
- Improve both quality of output and cost efficiency of the global CS organization.
- Ensure smooth operations of the global CS team with their available tools and infrastructure suite.
- Work with IT, Engineering, and technology partners as needed to refine the CS governance/operating model, holding each team accountable for experience, uptime (measurement and timely reporting), and delivery of new capabilities.
- Provide leadership oversight to ensure proper prioritization, impact measurement, and reporting across all CS programs.

In a nutshell, a CS operations function is the backbone for optimizing, scaling, and automating a CS practice. Having an operations-focused dedicated CS CoE can be a game changer to scale your CS practice, as we'll see in the following sections.

How Can a Dedicated CS Ops CoE Help Scale a CS Practice?

The biggest value of having a dedicated CS Ops team is that it brings dedicated focus, time, and attention to CS from an operational efficiency perspective. Typically, CS Ops starts as an offshoot of Sales Ops where the Sales Ops team runs reports, creates dashboards, and tries to provide the necessary coverage for CS needs. But their first focus is always on Sales and CS needs could take a backseat because of their other higher priorities.

In such cases, most CS teams adopt an ad hoc approach to fulfill their operational needs. CS leaders, and even individual team members, create their own dashboards, figure out their own metrics, and somehow get by.

In big CS Orgs, where the CS function also includes consulting services, professional services, support, and so on, having a mature operations sub-function like a CS CoE becomes imperative to manage the CS lines of business effectively and manage resourcing, forecasting, pipeline, analytics, and so on. Building a CS Ops practice the right way can make a big impact to your overall CS ROI and bottom line by optimizing operational and cost efficiencies and prioritizing and tracking things the right way.

Let us now look at some of the key areas of responsibilities of a CS CoE, as outlined in Figure 8-1, to meet the previously defined operational goals.

CHAPTER 8 ROLE OF CS OPERATIONS IN SCALING A CS PRACTICE

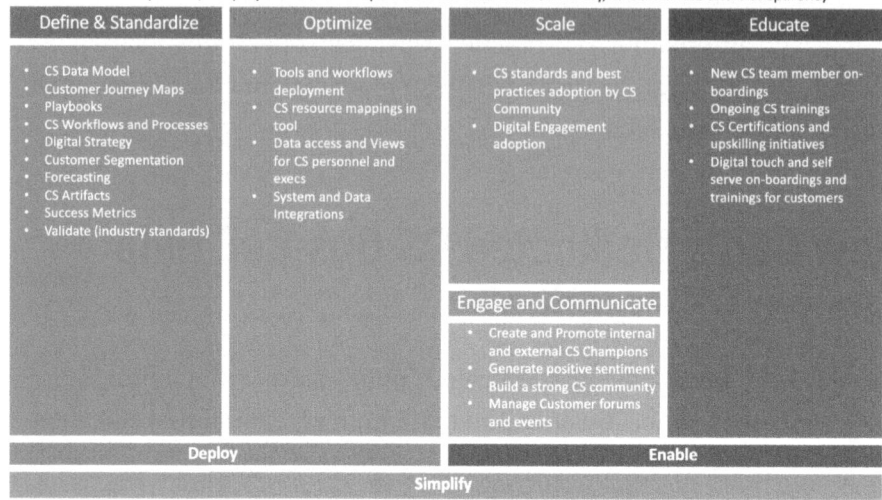

Figure 8-1. CS CoE areas of responsibility

Define and Standardize

The CS CoE is responsible for standardizing the CS practice by helping define the CS data and workflow models, including all the key processes, playbooks, journey maps, artifacts, forecasting, resourcing models, etc. Essentially, it defines the CS functional and scaling model.

Optimize

Once we have the workflows and CS Ops models defined, the next step is to implement and deploy them using the right tools and technologies to make sure that they are easy to use by the target audience.

The Standardize and Optimize phases are when the operational processes in a CS practice are deployed and maintained appropriately.

Scale

Once the right workflows, processes, and analytics dashboards are correctly deployed, the next step is to make sure that the deployed processes are used and adopted as intended by your broader CS community. Operations managers tied to different CS regions or business units within your company can help with that. Also, try to build a focus group of CS champions in different regions that can be your guiding star and source of truth to help you roll out better, standardized processes that your CS community needs and will benefit from.

Educate

It is also important to make sure that the CS community is enabled to properly use and adopt the methodologies, best practices, and scaling initiatives that your CS CoE team is rolling out. The CS Learning and Enablement team should lead that effort.

Engage

And last but certainly not least, it is important to make sure that your internal CS community of CSMs, CS managers, and other team members are excited and aligned with the overall vision and goals of your CS practice and how you are trying to fulfill and enhance those via the CS CoE. The CS community manager should drive activities like organizing road shows and CS community events, rewarding CS champions, and maintaining the CS community portal and forums to build and maintain healthy CS-community engagement and sentiment. This is especially important in big CS organizations with regionally distributed CS teams.

The overarching and underlying theme that should never be forgotten while setting up your CS CoE is the importance of simplification. Scale is never going to happen successfully if you don't keep things simple. Simple workflows, simple tools, and simple interfaces are key to ensuring that your operational, adoption, and scaling initiatives are successful.

Building a CS Ops/CS CoE practice the right way can make a big impact on your overall CS ROI and bottom line by optimizing operational efficiencies and prioritizing and tracking the right metrics and KPIs.

CHAPTER 8 ROLE OF CS OPERATIONS IN SCALING A CS PRACTICE

What Can Happen if a CS Team Tries to Scale Without Investing in CS Ops?

A Customer Success team trying to scale without a well-thought-out operations strategy is not an uncommon occurrence. Investing in CS Ops is, in most cases, an afterthought for most CS practices and not something many CS leaders typically plan for in advance.

Depending on the company, CS itself could be a very broad function encompassing multiple post-sales engagement teams, with its structure and agendas and workflows being very specific to the company.

Once processes and playbooks are in place, CS teams typically start off by the CSMs creating their own dashboards or using tools they are comfortable with to track their day-to-day activities. Some minimal organizational dashboards are put in place for the leadership. Often, a standard CS tool is not brought in early.

However, as the CS coverage and account portfolio grows and demand for CS increases, a realization soon dawns that the current ad hoc approach is not scalable. CS leaders do not have time to get granular on managing and tracking the CS metrics important to the organization. Information gaps start showing up, leading to chaos and frustration, both internally and for customers who start complaining about a lack of coordination within the company and inconsistent experience with customer-facing resources. And usually, that's when a company seriously starts considering CS Ops.

CHAPTER 8   ROLE OF CS OPERATIONS IN SCALING A CS PRACTICE

What Are the Blockers That Can Prevent CS Ops from Maximizing ROI from Their Role?

Some factors that prevent CS Ops being effective are

- Lack of proper structure in CS Org to aid operationalization.

- Lack of properly defined CS playbooks, workflows, customer stages, segmentation, etc.

- Lack of clear metrics to measure progress and success criteria and tie them to actions.

- Lack of strategic approach to CS for building a CS pipeline, CS resourcing, and so on.

- Last but certainly not least, lack of buy-in from CS and executive leadership on the importance of investing in a CS Operations/CS CoE function/team.

How to Maximize the Impact of CS Ops/CoE in an Organization?

To put it simply, what cannot be measured cannot be improved, and its value cannot be articulated. You can address this problem by making data your friend. Use CS Ops to help you better strategize, prioritize, plan, and build your CS Org and practice for maximum impact by leveraging timely, useful, and easily consumable data to create actionable insights. Adopt standard and repeatable workflows and processes to improve efficiency and scale. And invest in not just the operational efficiencies but also strategic projects based on region, business units, etc. to help maximize the impact of CS Ops.

CHAPTER 8   ROLE OF CS OPERATIONS IN SCALING A CS PRACTICE

Key Projects That Can Be Driven by CS Ops/CoE Team

- Voice of Customer (VoC) programs
- Data Consolidation and Analysis projects (C360, systems integration, etc.)
- NPS/CSAT surveys
- Customer segmentation
- NRR/ARR forecasting
- CS tools selection and implementation
- CS Resource planning and forecasting

However, a CS Ops team can only be effective if implemented in the right way, within an appropriate structure.

Structure of a CS Operations/CoE Organization

Where Should the CS Operations Team Roll Up To?

There is no definitive answer to this question. Some CS leaders would prefer to keep CS Ops directly under their wing so they have more direct control over the day-to-day workings of the Ops team's priorities and deliverables. Others might prefer not to take on the additional responsibility. Instead, they keep CS Ops as part of the broader Operations function within the company that also includes Sales Ops. That way, all the operations and enablement-focused teams can be under the same umbrella.

Irrespective of where CS Ops sits, as a function it should primarily be mapped to the Customer Success organization.

CHAPTER 8   ROLE OF CS OPERATIONS IN SCALING A CS PRACTICE

Structure and Roles

As mentioned earlier, CS Ops or CS CoE could either roll up to the Head of CS or roll up to the operations team with a dotted line to the Head of CS.

Hierarchically, one of the models could be implemented as shown in Figure 8-2. There is no right or wrong answer and there are pros and cons to both models.

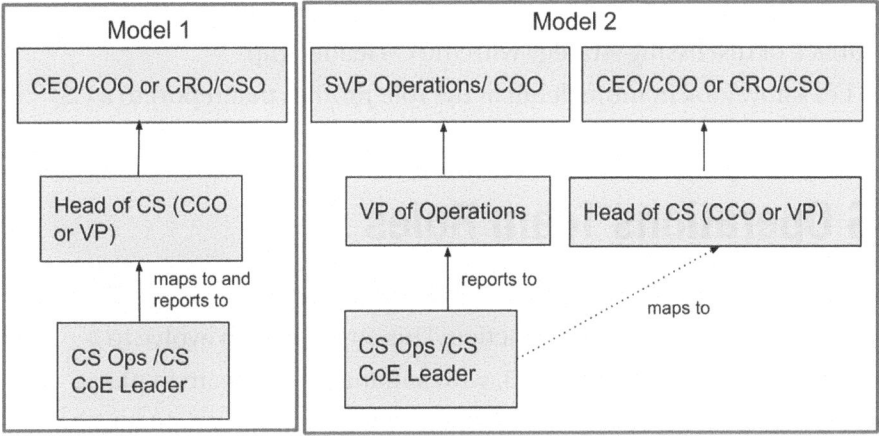

Figure 8-2. *CS Operations function organizational hierarchies*

If CS Ops/CoE rolls up directly to the CS leader, the CS leader will have more control over the CS Ops team's resourcing and priorities. And this is probably a good model to start with when the CS Ops team is very small. It would work directly with the CCO or VP of CS to get a complete understanding of the day-to-day workings of a CS Org and what is needed to support and scale the org.

However, as the CS Ops team grows, it would be an additional sub-function for the CS leader to manage. And the CS Ops personnel themselves could potentially become insulated and not have a holistic view of all cross-functional systems and operational workflows in the company. Since CS as a function is highly collaborative, and needs access to data from different systems across the company for workflows and

193

automations, having access to cross-functional systems and partners is key to their success.

Being part of a broader Operations team gives the CS Ops. team a broader perspective of what's happening operationally across the organization and ensures that CS gets a seat at the table for all key operational initiatives. Also, CS Ops/CoE being a separate entity from CS Org. could make it easier for Ops/CoE to have an objective view of everything CS is doing. It gives them an analytical lens when providing feedback or discussing strategy with the CS leadership.

Let's now look in more detail at the role profiles that report to a CS Ops/CoE leader.

CS Operations Team Roles

At its simplest, a CS Ops organization can consist of a handful of CS operatives mapped to the CS practice. This structure can evolve to a hierarchy, as shown in Figure 8-3, with a management team in place. Depending on the scope of the CS Operations team, you might require CS Ops. personnel with specialist skills like experience with different customer tiers, business units/verticals, and tools/systems to help operationalize robust and automated processes and workflows within that vertical/region/sub-function. CS Ops personnel can also be mapped to CS leaders in different regions depending on the size of the companies and CS teams.

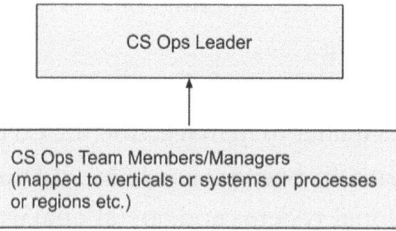

Figure 8-3. CS Ops team setup

CHAPTER 8   ROLE OF CS OPERATIONS IN SCALING A CS PRACTICE

For example, you could have dedicated CS Ops analysts for your CS sub-functions like Services, Training, Account Management, Consulting, etc., which will have different metrics to track, and different processes and programs to operationalize.

In a mature CS Operations practice with a full-fledged CS CoE organization, the org structure could look like Figure 8-4, where a CS CoE could have sub-functions and hierarchies focused on workflow development and standardization, tools and systems management, forecasting, program management, communications, learning, and enablement, etc. Sub orgs would divide the CS CoE responsibilities defined in Figure 8-1 among themselves.

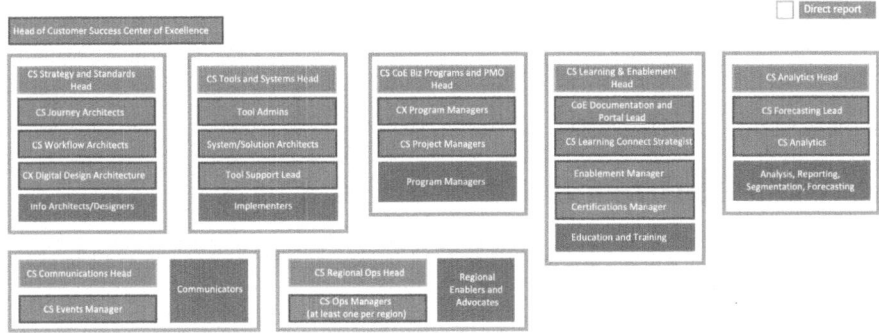

Figure 8-4. *A mature CS CoE org structure*

Irrespective of the reporting structure, CS Ops teams typically start with one or two personnel who are mapped to the Head of CS directly and grow from there once they have demonstrated value and ROI.

Let us now look at what a career trajectory in CS Operations might look like and how CS Ops leaders can plan the career evolution of their team members.

CHAPTER 8   ROLE OF CS OPERATIONS IN SCALING A CS PRACTICE

CS Operations Career Trajectory

While there is no one-size-fits-all, a CS Ops career path could look like the following.

CS Ops Team Member (Analyst/Architect/Engineer, etc.) → CS Ops Sr. Team Member → CS Ops Manager → CS Ops Sr. Manager → Director, CS Ops/CoE → VP CS Ops/CS CoE

Often, you would see the CS Ops. function drive CS Strategy and so the term "Strategy" would be part of team members' titles or job descriptions. Proactively driving CS Strategy should be a natural evolution for a CS Ops function as it matures to ensure that the CS team gets the most bang for its buck. This includes resource planning, ROI tracking, forecasting, metrics management, and building and rolling out initiatives like customer feedback surveys and customer 360 systems.

CS Operations Resourcing

The following are some metrics that the CS Ops. team can look at to justify its own ROI and growth:

- Productivity metrics of existing team
- No. of CS Ops personnel for every CS function or BU they support
  - Bookings, ARR per CS Ops team member
- How many leaders they need to support across the CS regions and ecosystem and how they compare to Sales Ops and other teams that support their functions
- Understand priorities for the coming year like new product launches, new teams that need help from CS Ops.

When you recruit, you'll need detailed lists of responsibilities for each position. To help you, let's take a look at some example job descriptions for a CS Ops function.

CS Operations Job Descriptions Examples

Example 1: Customer Success Operations Manager

Focus: Programs Management and reporting

<Company> is looking for a Customer Success Operations Manager to join our fast-growing Customer Success team. This role is responsible for leading the development and execution of strategic initiatives that empower our post-sales/win teams to provide an ever-improving experience for our customers. While the CS Operations Manager reports into <reporting structure>, you'll also work cross-functionally with the Sales and Finance Organizations.

This position will play a key role in managing voice of customer programs, internal workflow processes, and data integrity. Additionally, you'll leverage and analyze key customer data to increase product adoption, customer expansion, and mitigate churn.

This role is essential to scale our team in the most efficient and effective way possible through stellar communication, domain expertise, software knowledge, and the passion to continue to build our business!

Key Responsibilities:

- Collaborate with Customer Success, Customer Support, and Sales team to collect and understand our customer feedback.

- Organize and analyze customer feedback data by segment, product, and plan level to identify opportunities for new customer-facing features and improvements.

- Scale existing customer insight processes to create a cycle of continuous improvements for our product and close the loop with our customers.
- Participate in customer interviews to dive deeper into customer sentiment and areas for improvement.
- Conduct root cause analysis (RCA) workshops to understand customer churn rationale and motivations.
- Assign CSMs to new customers upon closed/won and assist with territory management.
- Evaluate and administer CRM/CSM solutions that enable CS reps to gain key insights and allow focus on opportunity areas among a high-volume account list.
- Support leadership to set goals, targets, measure performance, and workforce/team planning.
- Responsible for monitoring system performance, data integrity, and usage metrics.
- Act as the CS liaison for internal workflow automation, regularly partnering with TAMs, PS, and sales to ensure conflicting priorities are discussed and documented.
- Collaborate with internal stakeholders to implement and train the Customer Success Organization on new and updated workflows and processes.
- Create and maintain reports and dashboards for customer success/customer support teams.

Example 2: Sr. Customer Success Operations Manager

Focus: Programs Definition, Management and reporting, Sales forecasting

We are hiring a Senior Customer Success Operations Manager whose goal will be to drive the effectiveness and efficiency of our Customer Success team. You'll own metric definitions and execution, working to publish reporting and monitor key adoption, health, and retention metrics. Collaboratively as a key business partner for the CS leadership team, you will define the optimal customer journey and find ways to optimize our customer coverage model while making internal processes more efficient. A core part of this role will be to develop and scale the operational foundation and systems to drive the success of our teams, reporting directly to the Senior Director, Global Revenue Operations.

As a Senior Customer Success Operations Manager, you'll get to

- Manage renewal and upsell forecast cadence to drive accurate reporting to executives on past results and forecasts. Develop customer experience and customer health dashboards to drive decision-making and key focus areas.

- Track leading indicators of retention, renewals management, adoption, utilization, NPS. Develop analytical insights that drive recommendations for action around risk mitigation.

- Conduct market analysis and customer research to maintain a current view of customer needs, how to improve the experience for them, and what other Customer Success trends are relevant in the marketplace.

- Own metrics definitions across the Customer Success team, and the associated reporting and dashboards needed by team members.

- Define the optimal customer journey and advise the leadership team on organizing the team and defining playbooks to execute on said journey.

- Forecast and maintain up-to-date views of team capacity, and compare this to the optimal coverage model to determine hiring decisions and areas of efficiency gain.

- Own and implement account assignment and coverage model design and frameworks for the Customer Success organization.

- Define systems and processes that drive productivity, efficiency, and visibility across the entire Customer Success Organization.

You'll be a good fit if you have

- 4+ years of Customer Success experience at a fast-growing SaaS technology company – someone who understands what it means to be a great partner to our customers.

- Designed processes for scale and then realize their impact through your management of implementation and adoption across the business.

- Ability to break down ambiguous problems into concrete, manageable components and think through optimal solutions.

- Strong work ethic, desire to learn, and a drive to excel.

- Collaborative mindset across peers, business partners, and leadership.

- Clear, concise, and effective communication skills, both written and verbal. Ability to communicate the right level of information to executives and cross-functional teams at the right cadence.

- Strong analytical skills and comfort with Excel as well as GTM systems such as <list your preferred systems>

- Strong initiative and ability to work in a self-directed environment with a "can do" attitude and growth mindset.

- Strong interpersonal skills and the ability to negotiate priorities across organizations.

Example 3: Customer Success Operations Analyst

The Customer Success Operations Analyst will work on/oversee projects assigned to them each quarter to complete. You'll work cross-functionally with different teams to complete your projects and better streamline operational rigor across the department to set up the Customer Success org for success. You will maintain and implement new systems, create advanced reporting and dashboards, and automate workflow processes. As a Customer Success Operations Analyst, you will get an opportunity to work with different teams that make up the Customer Success org such as Support, Client Success Managers, Onboarding Specialists, and Fulfillment Specialists. This role will report to the Director, Customers Operations under the Customer Success org.

Responsibilities

- Work closely with CS Stakeholders to understand what projects and priorities they are focused on and immerse yourself in their day-to-day metrics/KPIs and workflows.

- Review current state of the data, organization configuration, and workflows being executed with sales and marketing technologies and recommend changes to the current usage of each tool.

- Provide weekly updates on projects that inevitably will help drive a positive customer experience, revenue growth, and operational scalability.

- Identify gaps to create new processes and own the project to completion.

- Implement/maintain systems.

- Provide reports analyzing the results of activities related to key business metrics to senior leadership.

- Assist with ongoing management of each technology and provide training and documentation as needed.

YOUR BACKGROUND THAT LIKELY MAKES YOU A MATCH

- 2-3 years working in an operations role required; preferably with a focus on CS Management/Onboarding

- Previous SaaS, CS, or sales experience preferred

- Proficient in Microsoft Excel

- Experience managing the following systems: *<list tools you use>*

- Demonstrates strong project management and organizational skills

- Strong operational and analytical experience

- Excellent verbal, written, and interpersonal communication skills

- Independent problem solver: open to taking instruction, but when needed, can independently translate a goal into an actionable plan

- Comfortable with ambiguity, and able to execute effectively

- Experience completing tasks and projects in cloud-based applications (e.g., CRM, project management software, Google docs).

Example 4: Customer Journey Mapping Manager

We are seeking a customer journey mapping professional, who will be responsible for researching our customers' journey to success across multiple use cases and industries, identifying friction points, gaps, and opportunities to accelerate their time to value. This is a customer-facing, high-priority role that requires excellent communication, organization, business, analytical, and technical skills. This Customer Journey Manager is responsible for leveraging data and customer insights to design improvements to the customer's journey to success. You will be a key member of the Success core team, and work on both short-term tactical journey changes, as well as longer-term transformational opportunities. This role will report directly to the Director of Global Customer Success.

CHAPTER 8 ROLE OF CS OPERATIONS IN SCALING A CS PRACTICE

Responsibilities:

- Own qualitative and quantitative research and documentation as it pertains to the success journey for our covered accounts, beginning with Large Enterprise (Fortune 500).

- Deeply understand our existing customers, their use cases, jobs to be done in a deployment, common pain points, and how business messaging can address customer needs.

- Work cross-functionally with teams such as Marketing, Global Business Solutions (Sales), Product Engineering, Partner Organization, Insights and analytics, and Customer Success Managers in the field.

- Document and demonstrate the current customer journey by developing visual journey maps which may include service blueprints, flowcharts, layouts, diagrams, charts, and models.

- Analyze specific success motion performance and make recommendations of ways to improve the effectiveness of our customer success life cycle.

- Oversee the analysis, reporting, and delivery of key program performance metrics of program to leadership and cross-functional stakeholders.

- Provide market intelligence and leverage industry best practices to continuously optimize and innovate our success offering.

- Able to act as a trusted advisor in addressing our customer's business needs.

Minimum Qualifications:

- 7+ years consulting, process optimization, research experience
- Proven customer interface and presentation skills
- Proven analytical, problem-solving, and creative thinking skills
- Demonstrated planning, time management, organizational, and interpersonal skills

Now that we have looked at some examples of job descriptions for CS Ops. roles, let's review the key concept of "CS Team Velocity," which is an important parameter for the success of your CS practice and how a CS Ops. team can help accelerate it.

CS Team Velocity in Relation to CS Operations

CS Team Velocity is an important parameter to understand both the productivity and effectiveness of a CS team. CS Ops. can play a key role in helping maximize a CS team's velocity.

If you establish a clear customer success velocity model and comprehensive CS processes by leveraging your CS Ops. function, you should not have an ongoing CS employee and customer churn problem that hits you by surprise.

Customer Success Velocity is a measurement of how many of your customers will achieve their desired outcomes with your product/service and how you service those customers with your CS resources.

CHAPTER 8 ROLE OF CS OPERATIONS IN SCALING A CS PRACTICE

There are only four primary variables that determine your Customer Success Velocity in any given quarter:

- Number of "ramped" CS members. In enterprise software companies, it takes time for a new CS person to ramp up and start producing. What counts is not how many CS reps you have, but how many of them are ramped and productive.

- Productivity of each CS member. Once a CS member is ramped, how much new business do they typically manage? Your CS organization's efficiency will be driven primarily by this variable. (Ideally, the productivity per CS team member should keep increasing for many years as your product, brand, and processes mature.)

- Churn in ramped CS reps. Losing a productive CS team member will impact your capacity, so you have to correctly model how many you are likely to lose and work to minimize it.

- Time to ramp a newly hired CS team member. That can take 2-3 months (based on your product and market and role). You have to correctly model this number, and simultaneously work to reduce it.

If you understand and carefully track these four variables, at any point in time you can calculate your productive CS capacity.

A Customer Success operations team should be able to put a forecasting model and a learning engine in place to track and predict a CS team's overall productivity, productive utilization of individual team members, and churn risk of employees. The learning engine should also be able to help the CS leader make decisions on when and how to maximize the overall velocity of the CS team.

Such sophisticated capabilities show that CS, as a function, is becoming more and more mature and, to a large extent, standardized. In the future, we predict that companies will start incorporating a strong Ops-focused approach from the get-go for CS, similar to Sales, as opposed to stumbling on the need to build out an Ops team for CS or being forced into it.

In this chapter, we revisited some of the themes that were introduced in Chapter 1 about the vision and value of a CS Operations function and a CS Center of Excellence and examined them in the context of scaling a CS practice. We looked at how a CS Operations org can be set up and its responsibilities. We also reviewed some examples of job descriptions for CS ops roles and also the concept of CS Team Velocity. This brings to a conclusion our discussion of the Core CoE foundational components.

In the next chapter, we will briefly cover the important focus areas for the CoE extended functions.

PART II

CS CoE Phase 2: Extended Functions

CHAPTER 9

Extending CS CoE

As Janice grew her global Customer Success practice and team at SoftCorp across different, geographically distributed regions, she ran into various challenges.

One was making those disparate teams, with their regional leaders and cultural nuances, feel like they were part of the same global CS community within the company. Another was ensuring that the new standards, processes, and tools released by the Worldwide CS CoE team on an ongoing basis were adopted properly by all the CS regions in a consistent way.

As SoftCorp expanded its business model to include channel partners to sell SoftCorp's products and services and to manage customer experience, Janice's CS team was tasked with training and managing the partner's Customer Success teams so they could offer their end customers the same type of experience that SoftCorp provided to its own direct customers.

Due to the growing scope of her CS organization, Janice decided to expand the scope of responsibilities of her CS CoE to support these additional requirements of CS learning and enablement, community management, and partner operations management.

Some of these could be key CS CoE functions that are implemented in CS CoE phase 1 (the Core phase), depending on the company type, product and customer profile. It's a decision that companies and CS leaders have to make based on their specific circumstances and requirements.

CHAPTER 9 EXTENDING CS COE

In this chapter, we'll take a look at some of these extended functions. If you follow the best practices and guidelines outlined in earlier chapters, you can easily extend your core components to include these additional responsibilities, and more.

Let's begin with an increasingly popular CS CoE function, Learning and Enablement.

CS Learning and Enablement

With increasing emphasis on customer, CS team, and partner enablement as a key differentiator in accelerating customer experience and customer's first time to value, CS Learning and Enablement is one of the fastest-growing sub-functions in CS.

> Enterprise software companies that have even a moderate level of maturity and product complexity have a dedicated training function as a key part of the customer success organization. - Gainsight

This function typically focuses on activities like enabling customers to achieve fast ROI through optimal enablement and education, building and maintaining training, and enablement and advocacy artifacts and portals for both internal and external audiences.

It also publishes ongoing training material for customers, partners, and internal CS teams on the latest features and products, and provides ongoing training to the CS team on the latest features, products, use cases, and trends. It creates and/or manages product and technical certifications for internal customer-facing post-sales teams and, in some cases, for partners and customers as well. Plus, it creates new CS employee onboarding artifacts and competency models.

CHAPTER 9   EXTENDING CS COE

Role of CS CoE

A CS CoE should be able to support a CS Learning and Enablement (L&E) Org. by defining and driving the right operational strategy to

- Vet and manage L&E tools like Learning Management Systems.
- Manage L&E workflows and operations.
- Manage metrics and analytics on usage and effectiveness of L&E artifacts and programs.
- Manage serving and auditing of certification exams.
- Track revenue from L&E team and help manage forecasting.
- Help set up the L&E team and define the scope of responsibilities.

CS L&E Metrics

The following are some of the metrics for consideration when building a CoE function for CS L&E. These metrics can be broken down per region or other parameters, as applicable:

- Number of Courses
  - Self-serve
  - Instructor-led
- Number of Programs (groups of courses)
- Number of L&E portal visits and views
- Number of Registrations per course
- Number of Log ins

213

- Number of Subscribed users
- Number of Course views
- Number of Certifications (if applicable)
- Number of Companies subscribed
- Number of Paid training sessions sold
- Revenue Forecast for training
- Number of Instructor-led trainings per region
- Number of Competency models (for internal teams)
- Time to first value (time between date of hire and end of onboarding for CS team members as well as for customers)

A key criterion for the success of a CS Learning and Enablement function is the existence of a strong CS community within your company, and a strong customer and user community. Without a strong community of champions and advocates, it won't be easy for the L&E team to effectively propagate learning and enablement programs for maximum impact. Building a strong internal CS community becomes especially important when you have distributed CS teams in multiple regions.

CS Community Management

Customer Success teams can play an important role in the management of a broader user and customer community. The CS Community Management and advocacy team's main focus is to build a strong base of internal and external champions and advocates for a company's products and brand while also propagating a strong internal CS community and sentiment in big, geographically distributed CS practices.

The scope of responsibilities of a CS Community Management function are

- Act as a conduit for a company's engagement with customers, partners, and internal CS stakeholders.
- Create and manage a broad user community via public or private community forums, blogs, Q&A sites, enablement portals.
- Conduct community workshops in different regions focused on increasing product and company awareness.
- Conduct User Conferences in partnership with other internal teams.
- Conduct Customer Advisory Boards in partnership with other internal teams.
- Build a strong internal CS community within big CS practices.

Many community management responsibilities, like workshops and user conferences are typically conducted jointly with functions like Product, Marketing, Sales, BizDev, etc. Having CS be an active participant in community management and engagement initiatives can be very rewarding because of the strong customer perspective and pulse they would have regarding customer requirements, use cases, and learnings regarding what resonates with customers and what does not. It's also a great opportunity for the CS team to get close to the broader user community of a company.

From an operational perspective, the CS CoE team can play a key role in the following ways:

- Managing community engagement tools

CHAPTER 9   EXTENDING CS COE

- Driving Customer Success-related communications with customers, partners, and internal stakeholders
- Managing and tracking end-user engagement via forums, blogs, Q&A portals, etc.
- Standardizing user and community workshop templates and agendas
- Tracking key metrics for review and analysis like
  - Number of Active users
  - Number of Comments
  - Number of Discussion threads
  - Number of Workshops conducted
  - Workshops ranking based on popularity
  - Number of Prospects from workshops – lead tracking (along with Marketing)
  - Number of CQLs – CS-qualified leads
  - Number of Customers attending workshops
  - Number of Attendees at user conferences
  - Year over year (YoY) trends of user engagement growth

If your company has a partner ecosystem, the Community Management team can also play a key role in facilitating communications with partners and partner's success teams.

Partner Operations and Success Management

More and more companies are leveraging a partner ecosystem as an extension of their own Sales and Customer Success teams. It augments their internal teams and extends their footprint to regions where their company resources are not available.

As companies leverage a partner-driven business model, they are realizing that partners have to be managed like customers in a strategically engaged manner. This maximizes ROI to both the partners and the end customers that the partners sell to and manage. Many CS teams are taking over Partner Management formally by assigning Partner Success Managers once partners come onboard.

The process is analogous to the Sales team closing a customer deal and then handing off the customer to the CS team. Similarly, the Partner journey is handed off to the Customer/Partner Success team once the BizDev team closes the deal with a new partner.

So a CS CoE should be prepared to map out the partner journeys and workflows and manage the portfolios of the Partner Success Managers, similar to Customer Success Managers. Partners can be of different types, like channel partners, technology partners, etc., with CS CoE engagement and workflow strategies varying accordingly. The CS CoE thereby evolves to a Partner and Customer Success Center of Excellence to provide the necessary standardization, optimization, and scaling services to partner teams as well.

The goal is to provide a consistent customer experience, irrespective of whether you or your partners are managing them. You should be able to leverage and repurpose a lot of CS CoE foundational components, like workflows, processes, tools, and dashboards for your Partner Success and operations management activities.

CHAPTER 9   EXTENDING CS COE

In this chapter, we reviewed the CS extended functions that a CS CoE can drive and support. In the final chapter, we will explore the latest and upcoming trends in Customer Success and make some predictions on where it is headed in the coming years.

CHAPTER 10

Where Are We Headed?

Customer Success has come a long way since it evolved into a full fledged function. From reactive to proactive, from tactical to strategic, from high touch to digital touch, it's been an interesting but not surprising evolution. We have come a long way, but in some ways we are just getting started.

They say that the best way of predicting the future is to build it, and that's exactly what we hope we've done in the previous chapters. We believe firmly that an increased focus on CS Ops. and the CS Center of Excellence is the way forward for all medium and large CS practices. And while nobody knows precisely how the future will unfold, in this chapter, we'll gaze into our crystal ball to bring you predictions backed by our own industry knowledge and the industry knowledge of all the CS leaders and practitioners who have contributed to this book.

We'll also look at trends that you can tap into immediately to make your own CS Org and practice a lasting success. They include the customer-centric business model, which we discussed back in Chapter 2. We'll start by looking at this and other emerging business models in more detail.

CHAPTER 10 WHERE ARE WE HEADED?

Emerging Business Models

As discussed in earlier chapters, we are moving towards a fundamental shift from product-centric to customer-centric and customer-led growth models, with an emphasis on standardization and scale.

Customer centricity is not a new concept. It means putting the customer at the center of your business model. You start by identifying the needs of an individual customer and building a product/delivery model to meet the needs of that customer everywhere, including the product, the marketing of that product, and so on.

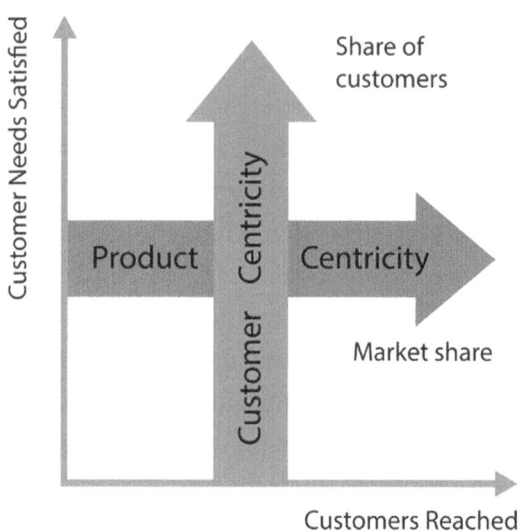

Figure 10-1. Product centricity and customer centricity

Source: www.linkedin.com/pulse/20130123164215-17102372-explaining-customer-centricity-with-a-diagram/

Most companies today follow a product-centric model, that is, they build a product or service that responds to a specific set of needs and look for customers who have those needs. The financial objective for a company that competes in a product-centric way is to optimize the value created by each product. In contrast, customer centricity focuses on optimizing the value created by each customer, as shown in Figure 10-1.

At the heart of customer centricity is a customer-led growth model that leverages data driven insights to derive value.

Customer-Led Growth Model

> *"Customer-Led Growth (CLG) is a strategic approach that leverages customer insights to qualify and quantify customer value, then operationalize and optimize the end-to-end customer experience."*
>
> —Forget The Funnel

The Customer-Led Growth Model derives from the philosophy of Customer Centricity defined by Professor Peter Fader in his book, *Customer Centricity: Focus on the Right Customers for Strategic Advantage*. Professor Fader advocates that in the world of customer centricity, there are good customers and then there's pretty much everybody else.

Strategies can be built specifically for good customers to maximize Customer Lifetime Value. So it's important to understand the customer segments and profile(s) that would benefit from a customer-centric approach and adopt a different strategy for them compared to the rest of your customers.

To put it simply, identify a subset of your customers (ideally some common customer profiles that you can extrapolate) who fit the top bracket of revenue and growth generators and put them at the center of your operating model (Figure 10-2).

CHAPTER 10   WHERE ARE WE HEADED?

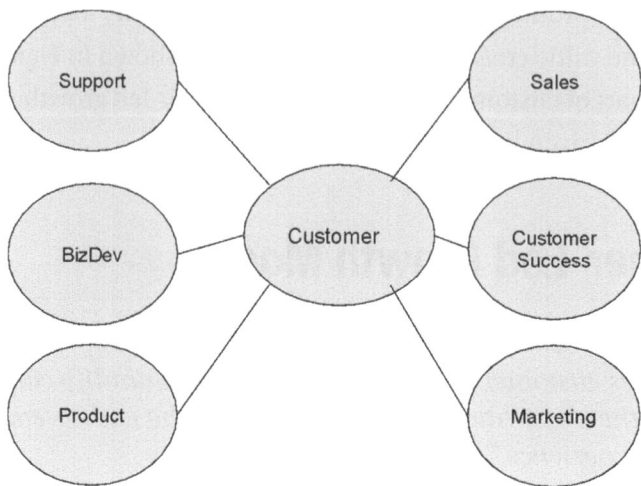

Figure 10-2. Customer-centric organizational setup

Based on the profiles you've identified, you can create an organization-wide understanding about the experience that is most appropriate for these, your company's best customers. Then you can decide on the marketing, sales, or product experience that fulfills their needs and the needs of similar customers. Instead of fitting customers into a defined product and operational mold, you mold your business and operations to suit your top customers. That way, you deliver value whenever, wherever, and however they need it.

According to advisors at Forget The Funnel, the customer-facing and technical teams in customer-led organizations rely on KPIs that represent value to customers and "rigorously qualify and quantify" that value. Doing this helps you understand "your best-fit customer and influences whether you implement strategies that are product-led (like Slack, Ahrefs), sales-led (like Salesforce, Marketo), engineering-led (like Facebook, Stripe), or marketing-led (like Buffer, Drift)."

CHAPTER 10 WHERE ARE WE HEADED?

While these models are not widely prevalent today, it is important to understand them. With the customer at the center of these business and operational models, Customer Success takes on a more central role in driving product and company strategy and in promoting customer loyalty and organic growth.

The New Era of Organic Growth and Creating Lifelong Customers

Organic growth has been a common model in many consumer-targeted companies, especially those like Google, Facebook, and others that follow an ad-based revenue model. However, many enterprise companies still follow a traditional growth and expansion strategy. The Sales team's expansion strategy revolves around identifying new leads and opportunities in new customer teams. Organic growth is treated almost as a nice side effect of having happy customers. We believe that is a missed opportunity.

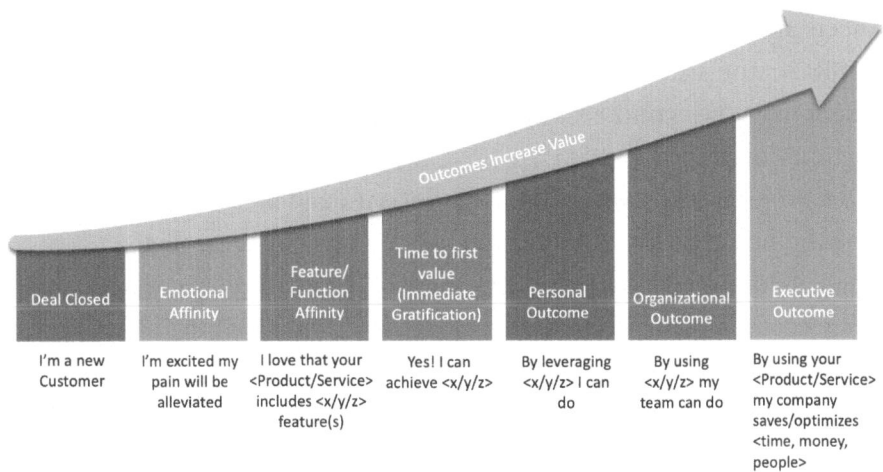

Figure 10-3. Moving from product purchase to customer outcomes

CHAPTER 10   WHERE ARE WE HEADED?

Companies should treat organic growth as an untapped opportunity and build a strategy to promote it by following the right engagement practices. Figure 10-3 shows how you can move from a product to an outcome-focused engagement model by following the customer's motivations and desired outcomes at each stage of the customer journey. Doing so requires a core understanding of the customers' motivations to purchase a company's products and how they are using them. And based on that, you build a strategy to influence growth.

A strong Customer Success organization, driven by the right set of priorities, can be the engine that drives ongoing organic growth, upsells and cross-sells for your company and creates lifelong customers. Customers stay with you and grow, not because you are constantly pounding their doors and beating the drum about your products, but because they want to be your customers. They will do business with you through thick and thin and consider you to be their partner and not a vendor. And that is a big, positive shift.

A strong Customer Success organization that creates organic growth is especially an asset to any company that is projects- and outcomes-focused. That's because the world is moving toward an economy in which projects are the main driver of value, according to an article published in HBR. Per the article, projects have quietly but powerfully displaced operations as the economic engine of our times and that shift has been a long time coming.

If a projects-based operational model is indeed the future of business, with everyone's roles within the company being defined by their responsibilities in different projects, then a CS team is uniquely positioned within a company to be part of this movement. It has a strong focus on desired business outcomes, delivery, project management, and customer experience.

Let's now look at some of the latest customer success trends and predictions for the future of CS.

CHAPTER 10 WHERE ARE WE HEADED?

Customer Success Predictions for a "New" World

It is hard to argue that today's business world isn't substantially different than it was a few years ago. Whether the parameters of this new, Covid-19-rewritten world are here to stay or whether there is some new state for businesses that's yet to emerge, you need to be ready. Even if the business world fully returns to pre-pandemic conditions, being ready to stay abreast of greater uncertainty and a deeper level (and faster rate) of change is a critical competency for companies.

One thing is certain. Organizations that survive and thrive in this new-normal will put the needs of the customer first. During the last 12 to 18 months, we have seen organizations with more mature and developed customer success practices realize faster and deeper insights. This visibility and knowledge includes understanding change at the customer level and recognizing potential strategic pivots that might help reorient the business. Customer Success can help protect existing recurring revenue, retain customers, and uncover new opportunities in times of upheaval.

We have identified six important changes that we believe will be a natural, evolutionary path for the Customer Success practice and will reflect our new reality.

Customer Success Will Have a Clear Path to the C-Suite

For many companies, Customer Success has evolved considerably from being an adjunct to a department such as Customer Service or Sales, to its own function with dedicated goals and resources. Some companies already understand the strategic potential of leveraging their Customer Success Org. to more deeply inform all parts of the business, uncover new opportunities, avoid potential pitfalls, and proactively ensure the success of each customer.

To maximize this access to valuable insights and resources, companies should create a clear, direct link to, and ideally a reporting mechanism between, the Customer Success Org and the C-suite. Many companies have already created a C-level role for Customer Success. After the upheaval we have seen in businesses due to Covid-19, and a general change in how customers are engaging, this trend will likely continue at a faster pace.

There Will Be a Substantial Increase in the Size and Scope of Customer Success

Naturally, with the elevated role of Customer Success and its value during turbulent and difficult times, Customer Success will likely not only have a direct line to the C-suite, but will also feature larger teams with bigger budgets and resources. In many companies, Customer Success could have a larger team than Sales. In particular, as selling and sales models change, Customer Success should take on a more substantial role by protecting against churn, increasing the revenue of each account, and promoting reference selling to win new customers.

As the team's role expands, it is important to find CS practitioners with the right skillset who can take on new capabilities or induct other functional professionals into customer success. In some cases, this will be a natural extension for the most adept employees. For others, companies will need to establish training and more prescriptive procedures.

For instance, employees may need more skills or training to take on upselling and revenue-expansion responsibilities. Many CS team members already do this to varying degrees, but they often do so in concert with Sales. If companies would like to shift the upsell responsibility fully to CS, then they would have to equip their CS team properly to set them up for success. In some cases, the customer success role may demand different or deeper skill sets than it did before. This might mean recruiting people a new skillsets for the role.

We also predict that more and more companies will increase the scope of the Customer Success function to include all things post-sales/post-win to provide a holistic experience to their customers. That could include post-sales account management, services, support, education and training. Today, in many big enterprise companies, many of these functions behave as parallel tracks to Customer Success instead of being under the same broad umbrella. But they all play a key role in ensuring that the customer is successful and that their experience is optimal.

Recognizing these functions as integral to a customer's post-sales/win experience and success and including them as part of the broader Customer Success umbrella under a Chief Customer Officer will help companies avoid competing priorities between these functions and help focus everyone's attention on the same overarching goal of maximizing their customers outcomes, experience and growth.

NRR Is the New ARR

Net revenue retention (NRR) has become a qualifier for funding and a key criterion for review at many board meetings. Previously, annual recurring revenue (ARR) was the focal point. We believe investors, executives, and the financial community are realizing that retaining customers and continuing to provide value to them is a more strategic measure and more accurately reflects customer and company health.

Net revenue retention (NRR) is retained revenue from existing customers that takes into account expansion revenue (upgrades, cross-sells, or upsells), downgraded revenue, and churned revenue. Companies will need to provide these metrics (actual and projected) to their finance departments, so it will be important to establish the means to get these figures updated on a regular basis. These are not just key C-level metrics; we believe they should be treated as core customer success metrics as well.

The focus on NRR and mapping NRR to CS is already happening in many companies and we expect this trend to catch on more and more.

CHAPTER 10   WHERE ARE WE HEADED?

Customer Success Leaders Will Need to Implement Customer Success Operations for Scale

This is another area where there is significant momentum currently, even if it's at a small scale. Customer success has historically been one of the few departments that lacks a plan for how to linearly scale its practice without compromising its existing value and the ability to take on new responsibilities. Headcount alone is not the answer. There are three important considerations:

- Being high touch
- Incorporating automation
- Reimagining technology

CS leaders will have to design a practice keeping customer segmentation, product complexities, customer engagement requirements and scale in mind. The key is to plan not just for the current scope of whatever CS may be handling today but for where it is headed, to avoid a total overhaul of processes at a later date. If the company expects to be successful and increase its number of customers, the CS team has to predict that growth and plan for it accordingly to avoid a potential disruption in its operations.

CS Operations-focused CS Center of Excellence orgs will become more and more common as the focus on standardization and scale increases in Customer Success organizations.

CHAPTER 10   WHERE ARE WE HEADED?

Lack of a Strong User Community Could Be the Trojan Horse for Customer Success

Initially, many customer success teams saw an online community run for, and driven by, customers as a support feature and a way to substantially lighten their loads. Now, community affects nearly all functional areas, from marketing to sales to development. Prospective customers often turn to communities to hear real customers' stories before committing to a purchase.

Sales can use a community as a facet of reference selling or can harvest prospective customers there. Marketing can use it as a forum for testing ideas, as well as boosting the brand and enthusiasm. Similarly, Customer Success should become more embedded and involved in these communities to ensure the success of their customers. Open-source companies like Databricks and HashiCorp have led the way in demonstrating how to successfully leverage a user community to support growth, provide self-evident customer references, and encourage the adoption of additional applications or modules.

If your company does not already have an strong customer community, Customer Success could partner with several other groups in the company, such as Support, Professional services, Consulting, Sales, Engineering, and others, to form one. New best practices like those outlined on *communityled.com* are emerging in terms of frameworks, guidelines, and best practices for leveraging this new growth tool.

Customer Success Will Have a Permanent Seat at the Executive Table

Given the critical role it can play, it stands to reason that Customer Success will take its rightful place as an essential business function with Sales, Engineering, Marketing, and others. This has resulted in the introduction and evolution of the Chief Customer Officer role.

CHAPTER 10   WHERE ARE WE HEADED?

The Evolution of the Chief Customer Officer (CCO) Role

Chief Customer Officer is a fairly new title and role in the business world that has taken off primarily in the hi-tech sector. There are many VPs and SVPs of Customer Success leading the CS Orgs, who could roll up to the CRO, COO, or in some cases, directly to the CEO. But recognizing the importance of managing the overall post-sales/win customer experience under a single umbrella is a recent phenomenon. It's a holistic approach encompassing retention and growth, services, support, consulting, account management, etc. And that recognition has resulted in the creation of the CCO role.

This role is currently more prevalent in small- to medium-size organizations, which do not have the leadership and resources to segment a customer's post-sales/win customer experience across different functions. The CCO role evolved because of the limitations and needs of such companies, but we believe that it is the inevitable future of Customer Success. Irrespective of company tier and size, the value of consolidating a customer's overall experience under a single unifying organization becomes more evident as the company evolves.

If the goal of a company is to be customer-led and customer-centric, then it makes complete sense to create a CCO role completely focused on customer experience, ROI and customer led growth. That way, they are able to maximize value and ROI, minimize churn and maximize retention and growth. If all the customer-facing functions such as services, support, and customer management have a common purpose and goal of maximizing customer value and experience, they will not get deflected or distracted from it if they roll up to a common C-level leader. Having a C-level leader who is measured on those metrics avoids sub-functions having competing or conflicting priorities of their own that are measured on an unrelated set of metrics.

CHAPTER 10 WHERE ARE WE HEADED?

"Chief Customer Officers play an increasingly important executive role because they are accountable for achieving important financial results while also connecting the dots across a range of mission critical customer-facing functions," says Rod Cherkas, CEO of HelloCCO and the author of *The Chief Customer Officer Playbook*. "They act as the cross-functional champion for internal initiatives that improve customer experiences and outcomes."

Cherkas explains that the role of the Chief Customer Officer has evolved significantly over the past decade in a way that dramatically expanded the scope and impact of the position. The CCO role has also expanded to new industries, including technology, financial services, hospitality, business services, and health care. "No longer is the CCO responsible solely for the strategy, design and execution of the customer experiences that make up what is often referred to as the 'customer journey'. That responsibility is certainly still a primary component of the job," Cherkas adds. "But now the CCO is also expected to operate as an executive level business owner who is accountable for driving financial results that significantly impact shareholder value. Post-sale leaders that can successfully combine their passion for improving customer outcomes with the management prowess to achieve this in a financially efficient and scalable way can become superstars."

Is the CCO Role in Conflict with a Chief Sales Officer?

The short answer is No! And it is important to understand that, to make sure that the CCO role is introduced, and received, by company execs. in the right way. The CCO's primary focus is on customer outcomes, customer experience and satisfaction, customer loyalty and retention, and upsells. It could also include existing customer growth. The CSO's focus is on company territory expansion, company growth, new logos acquisition, new products expansion, increase in new sales and related areas. Introduction of a customer-focused org should let the Sales be more focused on its core responsibilities and be a complement, not a competitor.

From CCO to CEO

In mid-2021, HubSpot's CCO was promoted to CEO of the company. And we've been seeing more CCOs taking on the CEO role. That is great news, not only for the evolution of the Customer Success but also for a company's general shift toward a customer-centric growth model. As the role of the CCO becomes more prevalent in enterprise and fast-growing companies, we expect this CCO–CEO transition to become more prevalent and established so it is no longer a surprise or a rare occurrence.

With the evolution of the CCO role and the increasing number of transitions from CCO to CEO, CS leaders are getting a seat at the table on their own company boards and are also being invited more and more to be part of the boards of other companies as well.

Role of Customer Success in Company Boards

Here is how Manjula Talreja, a senior CS executive at companies like Salesforce and Cisco and the CCO of PagerDuty, who also sits on the boards of multiple companies, describes her role as a board member.

> *Being a CCO is about focusing on three things: Customer Experience, Customer Outcomes and Customer Growth. The Customer Success group in SAAS companies has a direct impact on the top line of the company via Churn/Downgrade and Dollar Based Net Retention. As a board member, I make sure that I constantly bring that perspective to the table to*

drive key discussions and decision points. You must be focused on maximizing customer value and impact. This is extremely important; not only when you are presenting the value and ROI of your own customer success organization to your company's board and investors, but also when you are part of external company boards. Adopting a customer-centric approach is going to be a game changer for businesses keen on improving their customer engagement practices and customer-led financial growth models. And as experienced CS leaders with access to key customer data points and insights, we are uniquely positioned to drive this revolution from the front through our executive and board leadership engagements.

As more and more Customer Success executives become a part of company boards, the following are some tips on how CS leaders can approach their board assignments, discussions and presentations.

Be Clear About Your USP

Why should the board care about Customer Success? As a CS leader, make sure you have a solid storyline about what CS brings to the table and back up that storyline not only with data, but also compelling customer stories.

Focus on how CS impacts NRR. This would be of interest to the board and shareholders. Share an actionable plan about CS NRR mapping and targets and the plan to hit those targets. If CS is not quota-carrying, tie the CS activities like project delivery, customer engagement strategy, retention, etc. to NRR to show the impact the CS team is making for NRR targets attainment.

Have clear metrics for customer scoring, adoption, and other key KPIs the board are interested in and pair them with corresponding CS actions. Have stretch plans to challenge the CS team, since many board members view stretch goals favorably.

Last but certainly not least, generate positive momentum by highlighting something exciting about your future plans and what the board should look out for. Leave them in a state of anticipation. Think of Steve Jobs' "one more thing" moments during his public product launches and how that used to leave the audience.

Highlight Customer Stories

Often, the perception is that the board only cares about the bottom-line and numbers. Nothing could be further from the truth. Report on how CS is impacting company and customer engagement culture through better collaboration with cross-functional teams as well as with the customer.

Share customer stories along with hard numbers to appeal to the hearts of board members and not just their minds. Customer Stories are powerful tools in the CS exec's arsenal to really drive home the main points. The board should know that you are not just driving NRR but that you and your team really know the business and the customers. You know what they want and what makes them tick. That relationship based on truth and allyship will strengthen your storyline about the current and future state of NRR because your forecasts are coming from a place of knowledge.

For early-stage companies, customer learnings and insights are even more important where you don't have a lot of data to present. CS is the learning and feedback engine for the company and the board should clearly see that and appreciate the value.

Call Out How CS Impacts Overall Company Culture

How a CS Org helps change a company's overall culture to be more customer-centric and outcomes-focused to maximize customer ROI and experience is an important contribution and should be highlighted.

CHAPTER 10   WHERE ARE WE HEADED?

This should tie into your overall storyline about NRR and customer stories. Showing that CS helps foster a customer-centric mindset within the company is a key differentiator. It propagates empathy and better understanding of the customer by creating a tight feedback loop between the customers and internal teams like Product and Engineering.

So, considering the evolution of the Customer Success function, if you are a Customer Success leader today, or aspiring to be one in the future, how should you prepare?

How You Should Prepare

In this book, we've looked at the evolution of Customer Success 3.0 with a focus on a customer-centric approach to standardizing and scaling your Customer Success organizations and practices. We discussed the importance of focusing on operationalizing your CS practice by building your CS Center of Excellence, and discussed current and emerging business models, key customer engagement workflows, processes, metrics, and KPIs. We looked at ways to visualize, automate, and scale your CS practice for maximum impact and ROI by providing blueprints, templates, and examples. Finally, in this chapter, we looked at what the future of Customer Success looks like and the emerging trends.

Keeping all this in mind, let's look at how you, as a Customer Success leader or practitioner, can derive maximum ROI in your current or future leadership role by putting the right foundation stones in place:

- **Scope of Responsibilities:** Plan for expanded CS scope of duties, ideally to encompass all, or a large segment of, customer-facing activities once the sales cycle has successfully closed. Even if your organization has limited scope today, if your CS Org. is effective and able to show value, it is a natural progression to get more functions under your organization's purview to offer a seamless experience to your customers.

- **Measuring Success:** Have a clear plan of action for what success means for your organization and your company and how it will be measured. Even if you don't have a seat on your company board today, set the foundation stones in place for when you will be presenting to boards. Start documenting and presenting your CS results and stories to your current execs/managers in a similar way.

- **Focus on Automations and Scale:** If you have not done so already, take a fresh look at your existing CS operational workflows and processes and identify opportunities to automate and scale. Set the foundation stones for building out your CS Center of Excellence to standardize, automate, and scale your workflows and data design, even if you might not need or use all those mechanisms immediately.

- **Think Big:** Last but certainly not least, think big. The golden days of Customer Success are ahead of us. Don't be afraid to challenge the status quo, even if only in your own mind, and strive for something bigger and better.... because it is coming!

APPENDIX A

The Evolution of Customer Success

In the early 2000s, the software industry was beginning to move from enterprise, server-based platforms and/or floppy/hard/Rom disk-based delivery mechanisms. Software would be delivered, hosted, and accessed from the Cloud (called Software as a Service or SaaS). This move would become highly transformative for the entire software industry and caused the launch of a full-scale methodology of customer delivery strategies called Customer Success. Figure A-1 shows the customer success maturity model.

Customer Success Maturity Model

Reactive	Proactive	Outcomes Focused	Transformational
Manage escalations case by case as needed	Predict customer needs based on data and insights; turn data into meaningful actions	Proactively maximize customers desired outcomes at scale	Propagate a Customer Success mindset within your entire org; Customer Centric Approach

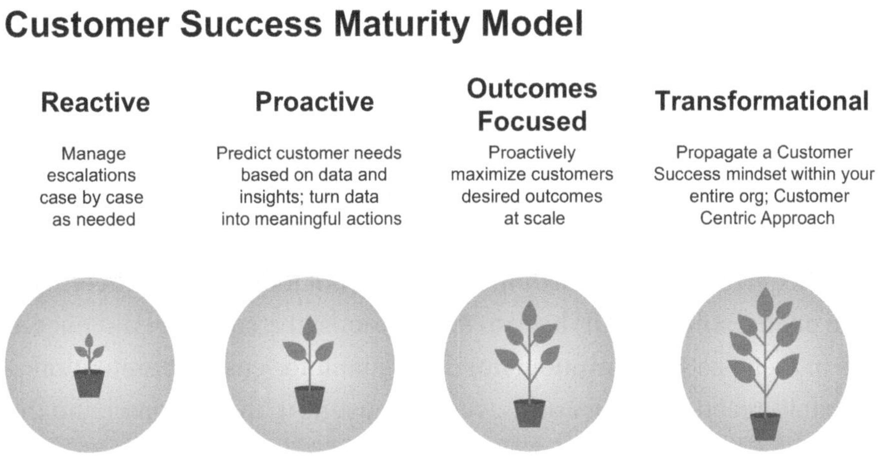

Figure A-1. *Customer Success maturity model*

© Chitra Madhwacharyula, Shreesha Ramdas 2023
C. Madhwacharyula and S. Ramdas, *Scaling Customer Success*,
https://doi.org/10.1007/978-1-4842-9192-4

APPENDIX A THE EVOLUTION OF CUSTOMER SUCCESS

Customer Success 1.0

The first iteration of Customer Success, 1.0 if you will, was launched with a break-fix philosophy. Customer Success' remit was solely to stave off churn and retain the customer. Whatever the cost. This methodology was more of a battlefield tactic where Customer Success would act in a concierge capacity, helping the customer to navigate the software vendor's processes and procedures. Customer Success would serve as a main point of contact for anything the customer needed and was the first point of contact for major technical issues that impacted the successful deployment or use of the software technology. When customers had major issues and threatened to churn, it was all hands on deck to solve the immediate problem and get the customers back on the happy path.

Customer Success 1.0 was measured on Net Promoter Scores, Escalation/De-escalation capability, implementation or Onboarding success, and Churn percentages. What "good" looked like from Customer Success team to Customer Success team across the market was not defined and no one team or service delivery model resembled another. Effectively, Customer Success' early days were compared to the Wild West.

Customer Success 2.0

Concierge delivery models and playing whack a mole with technology issues are expensive and only provide temporary satisfaction or resolution to the customer. Soon, the SaaS industry came to the realization that simply being reactive to a customer's needs is not the same as delivering return on investment (ROI) back to the customer, the customer did not see value in their SaaS subscription, nor did it guarantee customer retention. Ultimately, reactionary measures were exhausting to the customer and the SaaS vendor's team alike.

About ten years into Customer Success' existence in the SaaS industry, it would see its first evolution. Customer Success 2.0 focused on the delivery model. Focus would shift away from break-fix and lead with developing and maintaining a more strategic relationship with customers. Value realization and ROI delivery became the mechanism of successful customers. Business review processes, success planning, and strategic goal setting with customers were critical paths to ensuring customer retention. These proactive delivery methods were based on a single premise: Where the customer sees value in the SaaS technology, the customer will retain their subscription with said vendor.

Leaning into a proactive customer outcomes-focused function that we see today with a primary goal of ensuring that the customer does not become a churn risk and can make full use of their current investment to maximize their ROI.

Customer Success 2.0 is measured on Net Promoter Scores, Health Scores, Time to value, Net Retention, and Annual Recurring Revenue (ARR) growth. What "good" looks like from Customer Success team to Customer Success team across the market is much more mature and better defined. Purposeful and proactive customer delivery methodologies are more commonplace in the market.

Customer Success 3.0

Where 2.0 brought about the maturation of the customer delivery model, Customer Success 3.0 emphasizes a far larger and complex strategy on **scale**. Software manufacturers are still trying to answer the same question: How do we grow and retain our customer-base? There is no single answer to this question; it's likely there never will be. Customer growth and retention requires a holistic approach to customer experience delivery that unifies the entire SaaS company around the customer.

APPENDIX A   THE EVOLUTION OF CUSTOMER SUCCESS

To deliver a true customer retention strategy, the Customer Success function must scale beyond a team or a job title. It must scale through the entirety of the SaaS business from the product roadmap to data to internal and external execution. To drive that level of alignment toward delivering customer outcomes, **Customer Success 3.0 brings about a Customer Success Center of Excellence (CS CoE)**. The CS CoE should not be defined as a new team or set of job titles. Rather, it is defined as a unification of approaches to putting the customer at the very epicenter of the company's operating model.

There are a large number of functions within a SaaS company:

- Account Management is primarily revenue driven.

- Customer Success Management delivers a set of customer engagement "plays" to ensure adoption and ARR growth.

- Technical Account Management is responsible for the health of the customer's use case(s).

- Product Management defines new features/functions of the software.

- Engineering builds and tests the product.

- Marketing focuses on new logo attainment.

There are several other functions not listed here. With these many functions (each with their own remit and "North Star,"), how do you align each function toward delivering on outcomes for the customer and not inadvertently create a fragmented customer experience? The value of the CS CoE is to coordinate, orchestrate, and unify the delivery of customer outcomes.

Historically, we used to focus on customer satisfaction, experience, and retention in bits and pieces spread across multiple functions. In its ideal state, CS CoE is an all-encompassing customer-outcomes and experience-focused strategy, which includes services, support, post-sales account management, consulting, and in some cases, partnership operations as well.

Customer Success, in its evolution to 3.0, brings unified workflows and **standardization as well as results operationalization to maximize reach, efficiencies, costs, and customer experience**.

The biggest impetus and opportunity for CS CoE is going to be in the following areas:

- **Standardizing and scaling CS** with automations, tech touch, and process optimizations to all tiers of customers across a company to assure all customers realize value. The net result should be that companies have a better handle on how their customers, across all tiers are deriving value from their products and are able to use that knowledge to promote growth and expansion across all customer tiers.

- **Increased importance of CS operations** – which includes the metrics that need to be captured to measure company value and workflows effectiveness and analytics that need to be put in place to ensure an optimal customer experience and maximize their desired outcomes. CS Ops, for the most part, has been a neglected offshoot of Sales Ops. But with the increased focus and appreciation of Customer Success as a holistic and valuable post-sales/win function and its importance to all customers, CS Ops. is going to become a key differentiator and an important strategic partner to a CS org by helping capture and generate key data and metrics and providing valuable analytics and insights to affect a company's bottom-line; not only by helping increasing organic growth, automating customer churn, and health indicators but also by helping improve operational efficiencies and optimizing costs to scale.

- **Expansion of scope** of Customer Success CoE and Ops. organizations to also include areas like CS Learning and Development, Customer enablement and customer community development and management. This will aid a holistic customer experience model and strategy covering all facets of customer engagement.

- **Alignment** across the entire company to assure value realization to every customer. All team members should align on a single set of metrics and customer experiences to create a unified customer experience.

The first step toward a scalable approach toward Customer Success requires focus on CS Business Operations. Building CS CoE is the natural evolution of expanding CS Operations to scale across the entire organization and across all customers in a scalable repeatable manner, while maintaining a customer delivery model that delivers value to the customer.

APPENDIX B

Customer Account Team Roles and Responsibilities

Sales Rep/Sales Account Manager

- Co-account manager (along with CSM) if you are using a hybrid model
- Focus on account penetration, growth, and expansion
- Discovery of new use cases
- Build executive relationships

Solutions Engineer (Pre-sales)

- Focus on account penetration, growth, and expansion
- Lead technical discussions on discovery of new use cases
- Lead technical discussions on new features and future adoption
- Generate tech awareness about your company and products beyond current customer teams

- Own product roadmap alignment with customer
- Record customer feature and enhancement asks formally with Product
- Periodically review product roadmap with customer and provide updates on their product asks to ensure alignment

Post-sales Professional Services Team

- Own, manage, and drive billable projects and utilization.
- Work with customer to prioritize time and tasks (if needed) to enable desired outcomes and value.
- Document and track billable activities, status, and time spent on a weekly basis for easy review.
- Share monthly utilization updates with customer and internal teams.
- Drive technical escalations with Support if requested by customer.
- Help customer with workarounds or custom solutions.
- Conduct architecture and/or code optimization reviews.
- Share technical recommendations and best practices.
- Conduct customer training as needed.

Customer Success Manager (CSM)

- Co-account manager (along with sales rep)
- Build relationships with customer business leaders and stakeholders

APPENDIX B   CUSTOMER ACCOUNT TEAM ROLES AND RESPONSIBILITIES

- Understand customer's success criteria across different teams
- Deploy best practices for account management
- Send regular status updates to the customer and company leadership
- Drive customer Strategic Business Review (SBR) prep and execution (with Sales)
- Own customer retention and upsells
- Own customer experience and outcomes attainment

Common Responsibilities for All Customer Account Team Members

- Attend internal account sync calls.
- Create and share meeting notes with customer and internal teams after key meetings listing attendees, topics of discussion, recommendations or deliverables and next steps.
    - Ownership of creating meeting notes would be with the assigned owner for a particular meeting. There should be one owner even if multiple people attend.
- Document and track your tasks and deliverables.
- Contribute data to monthly customer status report, SBRs, and other discussions as needed.

APPENDIX C

Customer Satisfaction Survey Template

1. How likely is it that you would recommend this company to a friend or colleague?

Not at all likely - 0   1   2   3   4   5   6   7   8   9   Extremely likely - 10

2. Overall, how satisfied or dissatisfied are you with our company?

   - Very satisfied
   - Somewhat satisfied
   - Neither satisfied nor dissatisfied
   - Somewhat dissatisfied
   - Very dissatisfied

3. Which of the following words would you use to describe our products and services? Select all that apply.

   - Reliable
   - High quality
   - Useful

APPENDIX C   CUSTOMER SATISFACTION SURVEY TEMPLATE

- Unique
- Good value for money
- Overpriced
- Impractical
- Ineffective
- Poor quality
- Unreliable

4. How well do our products and services meet your needs?

    - Extremely well
    - Very well
    - Somewhat well
    - Not so well
    - Not at all well

5. How would you rate the quality of our services (provided by our Customer Success team)?

    - Very high quality
    - High quality
    - Neither high nor low quality
    - Low quality
    - Very low quality

APPENDIX C   CUSTOMER SATISFACTION SURVEY TEMPLATE

6. How would you rate the value for money of our product and services?

    - Excellent
    - Above average
    - Average
    - Below average
    - Poor

7. How responsive have we been to your questions or concerns about our products and services?

    - Extremely responsive
    - Very responsive
    - Somewhat responsive
    - Not so responsive
    - Not at all responsive
    - Not applicable

8. How long have you been a customer of our company?

    - Less than six months
    - Six months to a year
    - 1–2 years
    - 3 or more years
    - Free form questions

APPENDIX C   CUSTOMER SATISFACTION SURVEY TEMPLATE

9. What is one thing that you really like about working with us (any product feature, service aspects, any individual you'd like to call out). Please feel free to enter more items if applicable.

10. What are the areas where we need to improve to provide you an enhanced customer experience?

Glossary

CS: Customer Success

CX: Customer Experience

CS CoE/CoE: Customer Success Center of Excellence

BU: Business Unit

SaaS: Software as a Service

PaaS: Platform as a Service

IaaS: Infrastructure as a Service

Xaas: Everything as a Service

KPI: Key Performance Indicator

NRR: Net Revenue Retention

ARR: Annual Recurring Revenue

MRR: Monthly Recurring Revenue

ROI: Return on Investment

TCO: Total Cost of Ownership

CLV/LTV: Customer Lifetime Value

CPV: Customer Perceived Value

CLG: Customer Led Growth

SBR: Strategic Business Review

GLOSSARY

NPS: Net Promoter Score

CSAT: Customer Satisfaction Survey

VoC: Voice of Customer

RCA: Root Cause Analysis

CTA: Call to Action

L&E: Learning and Enablement

Q&A: Questions and Answers

GTM: Go To Market

USP: Unique Selling Point

CRM: Customer Relationship Management

CCO: Chief Customer Officer

CEO: Chief Executive Officer

CRO: Chief Revenue Officer

COO: Chief Operations Officer

VP: Vice President

CSM: Customer Success Manager

CSA: Customer Success Architect

TAM: Technical Account Manager

SE: Solutions Engineer

SA: Solutions Architect

SFDC: Salesforce.com

LMS: Learning Management System

YoY: Year over Year

QoQ: Quarter over Quarter

MoM: Month over Month

YTD: Year to Date

TBD: To Be Decided

References

Chapter 2

Closing the Delivery Gap (Bain and Company): https://media.bain.com/bainweb/PDFs/cms/hotTopics/closingdeliverygap.pdf

Chapter 5

Leading vs Lagging Health/Churn Indicators – Tom Lipscomb article: https://strikedeck.com/measuring-what-matters-in-customer-success/

Measuring Customer Success ROI - Eraj Siddiqui: https://strikedeck.com/measuring-customer-success-roi/

Customer Health Scoring: https://strikedeck.com/customer-health-how-to-score/

Chapter 6

Building a Customer 360 Dashboard

https://strikedeck.com/the-dashboard-for-customer-success/ by Dev Kurbur

Key Features of a Customer Success 360 Tool

https://strikedeck.com/

REFERENCES

Chapter 10

Product centricity and customer centricity (Figure 10-1)
   www.linkedin.com/pulse/20130123164215-17102372-explaining-customer-centricity-with-a-diagram/

Customer Success Predictions for a "New" World
   www.forbes.com/sites/forbescommunicationscouncil/2021/06/25/six-customer-success-predictions-for-a-new-world/?sh=259a9d662f70

Index

A

Account team, 20, 21, 54, 161
Advisors, 5, 67, 222
Analytics team, 5
Annual recurring revenue (ARR), 1, 25, 98, 101, 109, 139, 227, 239, 240
Anything as-a-service (XaaS), 2, 17–20, 88
Automation, 10, 26, 60, 81, 135, 145, 155, 170, 177–181, 236, 241
AWS, 17

B

Bain & Company, 28, 29, 104
Brainstorming sessions, 39
B2B business models, 16
B2B companies, 17
B2B hardware businesses, 18
B2C business model, 16
Business invests, 88
Business model, 16–28, 40, 58, 219–221, 235
Business philosophy, 120

C

Center of Excellence (CoE)
    components, 3, 4, 10, 11
    core functions, 4, 5
    core mission, 2
    departments, 2
    execution, 11, 12
    extended functions, 11
        Community Engagement and Management, 6, 7
        L&E, 5, 6
        partnerships operations, 7, 8
    goal, 3
    organization, 9
    prioritization, 11, 12
    requirement, 2
    role, 2
    set up, 2
Center of Excellence (CS CoE), 184
Change management, 7, 153, 158
Chief Customer Officer (CCO), 1, 36, 37, 227, 229, 230
    and CEO, 232
    companies, 230
    and CSO, 231, 232
    customer-led/customer-centric, 230

INDEX

Chief Customer Officer
    (CCO) (*cont.*)
  definition, 231
  evolution, 231
  functions, 230
  organizations, 230
  responsibility, 231
Chief Executive Officer (CEO), 15,
    37, 50, 73, 75, 230–232
Chief Sales Officer (CSO), 231–232
Collaborative relationship, 120
Community Engagement and
    Management function, 6–7
Company boards
  CCO, 232
  company's culture, 234, 235
  customer stories, 234
  executives, 233
  leaders, 233
  metrics, 233
  NRR, 233
  positive momentum, 234
Company leaders, 26
Company maturity, 22–23, 28, 29,
    32, 33, 37, 38, 40, 59, 63
Complex onboarding automation
    flow, 180
Concierge delivery models, 238
Consulting services, 42, 48,
    184, 187
Consumer-targeted
    companies, 223
Content management tools, 168
Core operational functions, 9

CRM tools, 56, 127, 162, 168
CS data modeling for
    standardization
  action plan for building, 160, 161
  customer data model, 158–160
  sample customer data
    model, 162–165
CS Learning and Enablement
    (CS L&E), 212
  function, 212
  metrics, 213, 214
  role, 213
  strong CS community, 214
CSM responsibility models
  account owners
    CS team, 70
    orchestration mode, 70
    R&R mapping to
      workflows, 71
    sales rep, 70
  joint account owners
    CSQLs, 67
    CS team, 67
    customer account, 67
    R&R mapping to
      workflows, 68, 69
    sales rep, 67
    Services/Sales teams, 68
  solo post-sales account owner
    R&R mapping to
      workflows, 72, 73
    teams, 72
CS Operations Center of Excellence
    (CoE), 184, 211

INDEX

CS Team Velocity, 205–207
define and standardize
    phases, 188
educate phases, 189
engagement, 189
Partner Success and operations
    management, 217, 218
responsibilities, 187, 188, 195
scale phases, 188
standardize and optimize
    phases, 188
team career trajectory, 196
team members' titles/job
    descriptions
    Customer Journey Mapping
      Manager, 203–205
    Customer Success
      Operations
      Analyst, 201–203
    Customer Success Operations
      Manager, 197, 198
    Sr. Customer Success
      Operations
      Manager, 199–201
team resourcing, 196
team role, 215
CS operations (CS Ops)
    activities, 185
    blockers, 191
    CS CoE, 184
    CS resource planning and
      forecasting, 192
    CS team, scale without
      investing, 190
    CS tools selection and
      implementation, 192
    customer segmentation, 192
    Data Consolidation and
      Analysis projects, 192
    dedicated CS Ops team, 187
    function, 187
    NPS/CSAT surveys, 192
    NRR/ARR forecasting, 192
    and practice for maximum
      impact, 191
    responsibilities, 185
    SoftCorp, 183
    structure and roles, 193, 194
    team roles, 194, 195
    team setup, 194
    VoC programs, 192
CS practice
    data and technology, 151
    people, 150
    PPT framework, 150
    processes, 150
Customer 360 dashboards, 127
    company-wide KPIs, 129
    components, 127, 128
    comprehensive customer
      health indicators, 128
    Customer Health
      indicators, 129
    KPIs, 130, 131
Customer 360 tools, 159, 167, 168
Customer account, 21, 39–41, 71,
    140, 143, 161, 162, 165,
    174, 184

259

INDEX

Customer Account Team roles and responsibilities
  common responsibilities, 245
  CSM, 244
  post-sales professional services team, 244
  sales rep/sales account manager, 243
  solutions engineer (pre-sales), 243, 244
Customer acquisition cost (CAC), 92, 97, 100, 101, 108
Customer-centric approach, 110, 221, 233, 235
Customer-centric business model, 36–37, 219
Customer centricity, 36, 220, 221
Customer-centric model, 220–222
Customer churn, 18, 25, 50, 69, 71, 73, 92, 198, 205, 241
Customer communication dashboard, 136
Customer data model, 126, 127, 153, 154, 158–166, 180
Customer education team, 6
Customer engagement
  models, 37, 158
Customer engagement tools, 167
Customer engagement workflows, 3, 7, 68, 149, 185, 235
Customer experience, 1–3, 7, 11
Customer health review dashboard, 140
Customer Health Score
  best practices, 95, 96
  data and analytics tools, 93
  evolution, 93
  formula, 92
  professionals, 92
  ranking, 93
  scorecard, 93
  scoring model, 94
  weightage, 93
Customer-journey mapping
  basic, 45, 46
  complex deployments, 47, 49
  customer outcomes, 46
  decision point, 41
  functional responsibilities, 47
  metrics, 108, 109
  post-sales/win customer journey, 43, 45
  stages, 43, 44
  value realization, 46
Customer-led growth (CLG)
  models, 36, 37, 220–223
Customer lifetime value (CLV), 40, 41, 91–92, 99, 100, 221
Customer loyalty, 1, 25, 96, 117, 126, 223, 231
Customer engagement processes, 149
Customer onboarding, 49, 171
  aspects, 75, 76
  bad onboarding, 50
  company, 77
  complex deployment, 66
  customer type, 77

INDEX

designing, 78
high touch, 77
key activity, 50
key systems, 80, 81
KPIs, 112
measurement, 79
metrics, 80
partnership, 50
planning, 78, 79
reducing time, 49
scaling, 77, 80, 81
tech touch, 77
tools, 167
tracking, 78, 79
Customer Perceived Value (CPV)
   article, 120
   CS, 117, 118
   CSMs, 117
   customers perception, 118
   formula, 119
   measurement, 119, 120
   monitoring/tracking, 119
   ROI/value, 117
   Services Teams, 118
Customer retention and expansion, 8, 24, 39
Customers, 20–22, 83, 102, 111, 116, 167, 201, 216, 223–224
Customer Satisfaction (CSAT), 26, 90, 96, 98, 130, 147
Customer's desired outcomes, 51, 96, 125
Customer segments, 135, 137, 221
Customer service agents, 172
Customer success (CS), 2
   churn mitigation, 32
   COE, 235
   community management, 6, 7, 11, 214–216
   considerations, 111, 112, 228
   CS 1.0, 238
   CS 2.0, 239
   CS 3.0, 239–241
   C-suite, 225, 226
   customer's experience/retention, 37
   customer success maturity model, 237
   data model, 127
   digital engagement strategy, 8, 9
   engagement models, 150
   evolution, 235
   executives, 121
   executive table, 229
   function, 187
   hierarchical model, 26
   key processes, 40
   KPIs, 130, 131
   leaders, 228
   leadership role, 235, 236
   life-long customers, 117, 118
   management tool, 167, 168
   methodologies, 15
   models, 16, 27
   operations, 4, 228
   organic growth, 223, 224
   organizations, 1, 7, 8, 55, 225
   pillars, 29, 30

INDEX

Customer success (CS) (*cont.*)
    company maturity, 32–35
    components, 30, 31
    relationship, 30
  practice, 124, 147, 148
  predictions, 225
  revenue tracking template, 145
  sales stages, 42
  scaling framework, 150
  scope and responsibilities, 40
  setup, 7
  size/scope, 226, 227
  strategies, 31, 32
  team members, 5
  teams, 5, 7, 8, 27, 41, 106, 229
  Team Velocity, 205–207
  tools, 166
  workflows, 40
Customer Success and
    Engagement model, 153
  data modeling for
    standardization, 154
  execution model, 156–158
  foundational steps, 154
  getting buy-in, 155
  tools and processes, 154, 155
Customer Success Architects
    (CSAs), 5
Customer Success Center of
    Excellence (CS CoE), 124
  alignment, 242
  company's operating
    model, 240
  expansion of scope, 242

  importance, CS operations, 241
  standardizing and scaling CS, 241
Customer Success (CS) teams, 229
Customer success managers
    (CSMs), 5–8, 20, 44, 55, 67,
    117, 119, 123, 140–143, 244
Customer success maturity model,
    22, 36, 237
Customer Success Qualified Leads
    (CSQLs), 67
Customer success tool
  customer data integration,
    133, 134
  customer workflows
    automation, 134
  specialized customer segments
    dashboards, 135
  streamlined customer
    communication, 136
  support report exporting
    capabilities, 135
  unified view of customer
    data, 132
Customer tiers, 19–21
Customer-vendor model, 20

D

Data Consolidation and Analysis
    projects, 192
Data-driven triggers, 125, 170
Delivery teams, 2, 76
Digital-driven automations,
    155, 170

INDEX

Digital-driven customer success, 151, 153
Digital-driven engagement model, 151–153
Digital-driven process automations
    customer's journey, 170
    customer workflow process automations steps, 176
    date-based triggers and milestones definitions, 173, 174
    digital customer journey, 171
    digital touch, 170
Digital/tech touch model, 19, 21, 151, 155–157, 170

E

Employees, 25, 26, 206, 226
End-to-end customer experience, 39, 221
Enterprise companies, 27, 77, 223, 227
Enterprise customers, 19–21, 60, 62, 64, 147
Everything as a service (XaaS), 2, 17–20, 65, 88
Executive dashboards, 137–138

F, G

Forecasting dashboards, 144, 145
Forecasts-tracking dashboards, 144

H

Hardware/manufacturing companies, 18
Health dashboard, 56, 123, 199
High Touch CS model, 19
HPE, 18

I, J

Ideal as a service (IDaaS), 45
Ideal customer profile (ICP), 77
Infrastructure as a Service (IaaS), 17, 18, 20, 65
Intelligent Swarming, 172
Internet of Things (IoT), 42, 47, 148

K

Key performance indicators (KPIs), 88–90, 99–101, 112, 113, 128, 129

L

Leadership team, 2, 52, 155, 156, 199, 200
Leading indicators
    business, 106
    conclusion, 105
    conditions, 104
    CS, 106
    definition, 103
    figuring out, 106
    KPIs, 104

INDEX

Leading indicators (*cont.*)
    *vs.*lagging metrics, 103
    measurement, 104, 106
    NPS, 104
    practical observation, 103
    users access, 106
Learning and Development team, 6
Learning and Enablement (L&E) function, 5–6
Lifetime value (LTV), 40, 41, 77, 90–92, 99–101, 130, 221

M

Manager dashboards, 138–140
Marketing organizations, 119
Metrics, 87
    churn rate, 91, 92
    CS, 99–101
    customer journey mapping, 108, 109
    executive, 87
    vs. KPIs, 88–90
    lagging metrics, 103
    leader, 87
    logical decomposition, 104, 105
    organization, 90, 91, 101, 102
    outcomes, 126
    process performance metrics, 107
    qualitative
        best practices, collection, 115, 116
        outcomes-driven, 113
        sampling, 113–115
    quantitative
        capturing, 109, 110
        company stage, 108, 109
        systems-driven, 110
    ROI, 97–99
    training, 102
Metrics-driven dashboards/reports, 11
Mid Touch model, 19
Minimum Viable Product (MVP), 9
Monthly recurring revenue (MRR), 91, 98–101, 105
Multi-pronged approach, 107

N

Netflix, 16
Net Promoter Score (NPS), 96, 98
Net revenue retention (NRR), 20, 26, 27, 37, 99, 105, 227
NewBiz, 25

O

Onboarding, 112, 130, 174, 178–180
Onboarding automation workflow, 179
Onboarding maturity
    adaptability/orgs, 83, 84
    communication/CX, 81, 82
    manageability, 85
    productivity, 85
    value orientation, 83
Open-source companies, 229

Operational management functions, 9
Optimization techniques
  business type, 59, 65
  company maturity, 59, 63, 64
  CS, 59

P, Q

PagerDuty's automation, 173
Partner Business Development team, 8
Partner-driven business model, 217
Partner journey, 217
Partner Management, 217
Partners, 2, 6–8, 35, 110, 151, 194, 201, 215
Partnerships Operations function, 7, 8
Partner Success Managers, 7, 8, 217
People, Process, Technology (PPT) framework, 135, 150
Platform as a Service (PaaS), 17, 18, 20, 26, 47, 179
Playbooks
  CSMs, 55
  CS playbooks, 56, 57
  escalations management playbook, 58
  purpose, 55
  standardization and templatization, 65
Post-sales customer engagement model, 37

Product activity score, 97
Product-centric model, 220
Product teams, 25
Professional Services, 2, 20, 26, 27, 65, 73, 98, 187, 229
Projects-based operational model, 224

R

Return on investment (ROI), 41, 97–99, 238

S

Sales, 15, 37, 39, 51, 124, 155, 197
Sales account team, 20, 21
Salesforce, 17, 25, 103, 134, 159, 163, 174, 222, 232
Sales/marketing, 37, 97, 229
Sales Ops, 183, 187, 192, 196
Sales rep, 41, 57, 67, 70, 165
Sales team, 4, 8, 24, 25, 39, 51, 67, 68, 179, 183, 197, 223
Sample dashboards
  CSM dashboards, 140–143
  executive dashboards, 137, 138
  manager dashboards, 138, 140
Sample digital-led customer journey, 171
Scale, 59–65, 150–151, 187–189, 239
Services teams, 101, 118
Sleeter Group, 103
SoftCorp, 1, 39, 183, 211

INDEX

Software as a service (SaaS), 16, 17, 20, 109
Spenders, 21
Stakeholders, 2, 39, 52, 82, 96, 115, 125, 158, 172, 198
Standard automation process, 175
Startups
    early-stage
        companies, 24
        customers, 24
        investments, 24
        structure, 25
    late-stage, 27, 28
    mid-stage, 26, 27
Strategic account planning, 51
    applications, 55
    CS tools, 51
    features, 54
    tasks, 54
    teams, 51
    templates, 51–55
    use cases, 55
Strategic business review (SBR), 56
Strategic customers, 20
Suppliers, 120
Support teams, 6, 102
Support tools, 168
Survey tools, 167

T

Technical Account Managers (TAM), 70, 198
Technical support, 177
Time to Live (TTL), 98
Tools and Systems team, 5
Total Contract Values (TCV), 24
Toyota, 120
Traditional on-prem business models, 18

U, V

Unified customer data model, 127, 158, 160, 180

W, X, Y, Z

World-class experience, 1

The manufacturer's authorised representative in the EU is Springer Nature Customer Service Centre GmbH, Europaplatz 3, 69115 Heidelberg, Germany. If you have any concerns regarding our products, please contact ProductSafety@springernature.com

Printed and bound by CPI Group (UK) Ltd, Croydon, CR0 4YY

23/03/2026

02076398-0008